Swing, Hard Bop, Bop & Bebop

Biographical Jazz Prose Poems

By

Horace Mungin

SWING, HARD BOP, BOP & BEBOP

HORACE MUNGIN

Swing, Hard Bop, Bop & Bebop by Horace Mungin, © Copyright 2018 Horace Mungin. All Rights Reserved and Preserved. No part of this book may be reproduced or transmitted in any form or by any means, electronic or mechanical, including photocopying, recording, or by information storage and retrieval systems, without written permission of the Publisher with exceptions as to brief quotes, references, articles, reviews, and certain other noncommercial uses permitted by copyright law.

For Permission requests, write to:

YBR Publishing
c/o J&C Wordsmiths LLC
PO Box 4904
Beaufort SC 29903-4904
contact@ybrpub.com
843-597-0912

SWING, HARD BOP, BOP & BEBOP

HORACE MUNGIN

ISBN- 0-9980582-7-0
ISBN-13: 978-0-9980582-7-6

Cover art by Hampton Olfus
Cover design and interior formatting by Jack Gannon - www.ybrpub.com

SWING, HARD BOP, BOP & BEBOP

Dedicated To
Akbar Ernest Ellis

SWING, HARD BOP, BOP & BEBOP

HORACE MUNGIN

Cover Art
~Many Thanks to Hampton Olfus

SWING, HARD BOP, BOP & BEBOP

Also By Horace Mungin

Sleepy Willie Talks About Life
Sleepy Willie Sings the Blues
The Devil Beats His Wife
San Juan Hill
Subway: After the Irish
Poetic Portraits: The African People of San Juan Hill
A Different Point of View
Truth & Absurdities
...Or Does It Explode

These books can be ordered at:
www.horacemunginbooks.com
(843) 437-7567

**Horace Mungin Books
152 McArn Road
Ridgeville, SC 29472
(843) 875-3886**

SWING, HARD BOP, BOP & BEBOP

HORACE MUNGIN

*You can't play music and
work at the Post Office*

~Thelonious Monk

SWING, HARD BOP, BOP & BEBOP

Publisher's Note

At the end of most chapters is a QR Code that links to a random YouTube page which exemplifies the music of the artist discussed. Using the QR Reader app on an iPhone or Smartphone will allow the reader to experience the music while reading about the artist!

These links are not endorsements of individual YouTube channels, as there are many channels with each song linked in these pages. These links direct the reader to the author's playlist.

SWING, HARD BOP, BOP & BEBOP

Contents

The History of New Music in America	23
Jazz	24
Syncopation	25
52nd Street	26
Birdland	27
Minton's Playhouse	29
The Jazz Mobile	30
The Apollo Theater	31
Grant's Tomb	32
William (Pee Wee) Marquette	33
Symphony Sid	34
Marian McPartland	36
Louis Armstrong	38
Duke Ellington	41
William Count Basie	43
John Hammond	45
Ella Fitzgerald	48
Joe Williams	50
John Gillespie	52
Charlie Parker	54
Lester Young	57
Billie Holiday	59
Coleman Hawkins	62
Ben Webster	63
Bud Powell	65
King Pleasure	67
Miles Davis	68
Art Blakey	70
Horace Silver	72

SWING, HARD BOP, BOP & BEBOP

Charlie Mingus	74
Oscar Peterson	76
Gerry Mulligan	78
Cannonball Adderley	80
John Coltrane	82
Coltrane Talks to God	84
Thelonious Monk	86
Thelonious Monk on Amsterdam Avenue	89
Baroness Pannonica de Koenigswarter	91
Thelonious Sphere Monk	93
Max Roach	94
Ahmad Jamal	96
Nina Simone	98
One Woman	99
Eddie Harris	100
Sarah Vaughn	101
Sun Ra	102
Dexter Gordon	104
Sonny Rollins	106
Paul Desmond	108
Hank Mobley	109
Lee Morgan	110
Wes Montgomery	111
Rahsaan Roland Kirk	113
Les McCann	115
Herbie Hancock	117
Red Garland	119
Abbey Lincoln	121
Stan Getz	122
George Shearing	124
Pharoah Sanders	125
A Tribute to Teo Macero	127

HORACE MUNGIN

Author's Note

I was raised in a neighborhood with a long involvement in the creation, celebration and unconventional embracing of music – jazz music. San Juan Hill was a 4-block area on mid-Manhattan's West Side; 60th to 64th Streets, Amsterdam to West End Avenues, in New York City. San Juan Hill was one of the largest black neighborhoods in Manhattan before the rise of Harlem. The Neighborhood was named to honor the United States Army's black 10th Cavalry, which fought at the battle of San Juan Hill during the Spanish-American War in 1898. San Juan Hill's fire-prone, monotonous tenements were the worst type of housing which the city allowed to stand. The entire area was plagued by regular fires caused by cooking with hot plates. Up to 5,000 people lived jammed into a single block; the tenement buildings were mostly four floor structures with four to six single or double room units on a floor, one bathroom per floor, beds were often used in shifts, shared by boarders.

San Juan Hill's streets were lined with gritty tenements, but there was a vibrant jazz scene; ground floor apartments were turned into illegal underground speakeasies with player pianos, but often with live music provided by local talents. Every block had one or two such establishments. Nearly all of the establishments had a piano, Willie (the Lion) Smith played in some of the better attended parlors. The keyboard style that bridged the idioms of classic ragtime and jazz was known as stride piano of which Willie the Lion was a master. James P. Johnson played in the Jungle's Casino where he wrote the tunes that turned into the Charleston, the biggest dance craze of the twentieth century.

These gin and jazz joints flourished until 1907 when Mary White Ovington, a white progressive social worker convinced a group of liberal philanthropists to build the Phipps Houses to stem the migration of Negroes from San Juan Hill to Harlem. The Phipps Houses were a delightful new addition to this neighborhood of run-down scarred tenements with one bathroom per floor where tenets had to cook on hot plates. The six story Phipps, built at the end of 63rd and 64th Streets, was steam heated and fireproof; each apartment had running water, a bathroom and a kitchen, there was also a roof garden in each building and a courtyard.

Some of the gin and jazz joints lasted beyond this period; up to the late 1940's when the area was torn down to build the Amsterdam City Housing – the Projects. The family of Thelonious Monk moved into the Phipps Houses in 1922 while most of these joints still operated and Monk was raised there –

it was there that he first heard stride piano. In the late 40's when the Projects were built nearly all of the remaining joints that featured music vanished; only on 61st Street was there still a few after-hour gin joints that also operated as numbers holes. Many of the local musicians who lived in either the Phipps Houses or the Amsterdam Projects had to find work in Harlem or Greenwich Village.

The projects officially opened in 1948. My family arrived there in 1950. Thelonious Monk was, by then, a well-known jazz musician and one of the creators of bebop. Many of the neighborhood talents were eager to duplicate Monk's success, music was everywhere, Jazz was the music of choice for San Juan Hill although there was a strong following for doo wop and Latin music because of the growing Puerto Rican population. Groups of young people formed friendships around which music they preferred. Each group type-casted their group as the real music aficionados and the others they type casted in distinctive unflattering categories.

In the mid 50's I was firmly into the jazz camp. We saw ourselves as cool, perceptive, hip bohemians – the future. John Coltrane was our sage; Sonny Rollins was our priest and Miles Davis was our deity. The group of young teenagers that I hung out with attended neighborhood weekend house parties where do wop and R & B was king, but when we were alone as a group of two or more, we revered jazz, we listened to jazz, we talked jazz – jazz was our all in all. Other teens collected baseball cards and kept up on hit/run statistics, my group kept up on what jazz musician was in town –who was at Birdland, we knew the list of sidemen, we knew who played bass or drums with which major headliner. We rated who was top on tenor, baritone and alto sax. There was, for us, little doubt about who was king on trumpet and drums – these were the statistics we kept. I would meet with various grouping of my friends and we listened to their father's records. One of my friend's father had a 6-track tape recorder with lots and lots of Art Blakey's Jazz Messengers music. At another friend's house whose father favored Ahmad Jamal, we would listen to his rendition of *Poinciana* with our eyes closed and in dead silence – no one dared break the mood by speaking.

We may have even been a bit snooty in our thinking that we displayed better judgements by our ability to appreciate the more sophisticated form of music. We didn't consider other forms of music as simply another genre that could be enjoyed for its own merits, we thought of other forms of music as blasphemy - I was in my thirties before I could appreciate James Brown.

Chained Africans started the tradition of African American music on the slave ships headed to Gadsden's Wharf in Charleston, South Carolina by sending out an exalting wail beseeching God's mercy for something to protect and fortify them from the anticipated centuries of bondage and tyranny. On land, a generation later, those wails developed into field hollers and work songs that gave slave laborers a transcendental boost that carried them upright all day until they could, deep in the night, lay their bodies down. Those work songs matured into spirituals songs that further fortified the slave's supernatural will to survive, plus these work songs included coded instructions on how to escape and how to read the starry map of the sky to reach the freedom of the north. Indeed, some of those songs pulled double duty by encouraging sovereignty and giving directions on how to escape north – "*Follow the Drinkin' Gourd.*" From this point on, black music would forever carry elements that were only understood by black people.

We heard Monk and Charlie Rouse rehearsing live some Saturday morning as their music sailed from Monk's open window over to the basketball court around the corner from 238 West 63rd street where Monk lived in the Phipps Houses. We often saw jazz musicians walking in the neighborhood on their way to Monk's crib.

We lived slightly more than a half mile from the famed 52nd Street that seem like some mythical musical kingdom to us with enchanting clubs where our idols sermonized canons of life; and music stores with all kinds of instruments tastefully hanging in their windows enhanced by sheet music placed randomly among the instruments. Manny's Music store was our favorite and it was where I bought my first flute. Many of my associates wanted to become jazz musicians and one by one, as we got the money, we went to Manny's to buy the instrument of our choice.

We had to past 52nd Street on our trips to the movie theaters on 42nd Street – in good weather we walked. Before I purchased the flute, I would always stop by Manny's and gaze at the three flutes in the store window displayed among the other instruments; one hanging from a wire and two others all put together and resting on their red velvet lined cases.

A neighborhood guy who played the flute taught me how to get a sound from the mouthpiece and how to properly hold the assembled instrument, but he moved before we got much further in my lessons. I learned on my own by playing along with recordings by Herbie Mann and Yusef Lateef, but I never received any musical training, in my case, a sure recipe for failure. My consolation prize was that I had an understanding and an appreciation for the only high art form invented on American soil. I have been enjoying jazz and its evolution all of my life. The next best thing to being a jazz musician.

A special, gifted and select group of (mostly) black men came together to create a music and an environment that influenced much of the world's humanity. These men and their music flourished for half a century. These African American men used European instruments to invent the next movement in the evolution of the music that expresses the history of an enslaved African people. They created an important portion of black culture that was shared with the world. While the era was unique and never to be repeated, it was also merely a link in the evolution of black music.

It is this life-long association with jazz music and my eternal appreciation of it that prompts this book. I wish that I could have included every person who ever played jazz in this book. My biggest regret is that there are so many fine jazz musicians missing from the pages of this book. My method of selection was more instinctive than systematic. My original intention was to highlight the musicians who, in my mind, were masters of bebop and those who were the stars that made 52nd Street shine. This book does that, but there are as many fine jazz artists missing from the book as there are in it.

This same thing is true when it comes to jazz venues. Jazz aficionados will wonder aloud what about this or that club where they have fond memories of seeing this or that artist. I admit a fuller account of jazz venues would have delivered a more satisfying story of jazz's golden age.

All that being what it is this book is still the most significant condensed description of the bebop era and its practitioners available today.

The History of New Music in America

The first Africans upon the slave ships destined
For the Americas sensed the coming of
A great and lasting catastrophe
They had nothing that would
Protect and fortify them
From the coming centuries of bondage and tyranny
So they sent out an exalting wail
Beseeching God's mercy
God looked down on them and saw
That they had nothing
They were naked and in chains
God in His singular wisdom
Took the very sound of their lament
And turned it into their shield and their weapon
And today we call that sound music
It is those majestic wails
Those cries of despair
That music
In its ever-changing forms
From field holler to hip-hop
That has nourished our spirits through the centuries
A sound that spoke directly to On-high
For sustenance to keep the spirit
Unyielding to the horrors of shackled burdens
Feeble and conquered, music
Became our sacred shield
And our consecrated weapon.

SWING, HARD BOP, BOP & BEBOP

Jazz

Hey baba Rebop
Baba Rebop
Cut a rug
Jitterbug
Boogie
Boogie Woogie
Rag Mop
Pooper stopper
Bugaloo
Rusty Dusty
Bebop
Sporty Oddity
Hip-Hop
Didity Bopper
Rag Mop
Bebop
Hip-Hop.

Syncopation
(For Patti)

Pure grace is her every
Gesture

A wave, a shrug, a nod
All movements of elegant poise
Motion syncopation

Scott Joplin's sound
Lives when she moves…and
Awkwardness begs mercy.

SWING, HARD BOP, BOP & BEBOP

52nd Street

The original "Swing Street" was 133rd Street
Between Seventh and Lenox Avenues in Harlem
As many as 20 clubs – prohibition speakeasies where
The mingling of the races earned it the name "Jungle Alley"
The clubs all had a Chicago gangland atmosphere and
With the repeal of prohibition and the 1935 uprising
The white money behind the clubs showed up on 52nd Street
Downtown where jazz clubs were opened almost monthly

52nd Street between Fifth and Seventh Avenues squeezed
Together more than 30 clubs in the basements or main floors
Of tenement buildings from the nineteenth century turned
Themselves into café's and eateries of all descriptions
But the main attraction was music, After Minton's Playhouse
In Harlem, 52nd Street was the second most important
Distributor of bebop, Symphony Sid broadcasted live
From 52nd Street, there isn't anyone who played jazz in
That era that did not appear on 52nd Street is the easiest
Way to list who appeared there

The brightly lit marquees rivaled that of Broadway
And the theater district with names that offered
Far more exciting attractions like in Paris or heaven

Monk wrote a tune in honor of the street called
"52nd Street Theme" that became the bebop anthem that
Was performed by artists at the clubs, actor/director Clint
Eastwood made a movie about the street and the clubs and
The era called "Bird" these poems are about that street and
The jazz artists who made the clubs swing, the neighborhood
Started to change in the late fifties and the clubs closed one
By one until the last one folded in 1968 and Swing Street was
No more, only sweet, sweet memories of, oh what a time.

HORACE MUNGIN

Birdland

Named to take advantage of the popularity
Of its star house performer, Birdland was
Billed as the home of Charlie Yardbird Parker
Who didn't appear there as often as the house
And the fans would have wanted him too
Money was always the reason

December 15, 1949 – opening night – with Charlie
Yardbird Parker, Lester Prez Young, Harry Belafonte
And Stan Getz, a monumental jazz history at Birdland
From the getup the club's allure attracted other musicians
Like Art Blakey who recorded the album
"A Night at Birdland" and John Coltrane who recorded
His "Live at Birdland" there, they all wanted to appear at Birdland

The master of ceremonies was a diminutive Alabamian
Named William Pee Wee Marquette whose voice was so
High-pitched some thought him female, Pee Wee was
Notorious for mispronouncing musician's names when
He introduced them if they hadn't tipped him

Birdland quickly became the fashionable place to be seen
With regulars like Frank Sinatra and wife Ava Gardner,
Gary Cooper, Marilyn Monroe, Sugar Ray Robinson
Marlene Dietrich, Joe Louis and Judy Garland
But quiet as it was kept, Birdland's owner Irving Levy
Was stabbed to death at the club December 1959

The real scandal occurred at Birdland in August 1959
When Miles Davis walked a pretty white girl outside the
Club and hailed a cab for her – a white cop came up to Miles
And ordered him to "move on" Miles pointed to the marquee
"I'm working here, that's my name you see there"
The cop told Miles he didn't care where he worked
He had to move on – Miles just stared at him, other cops
Came to the scene and a scuffle broke out, Miles had
Been doing some gym boxing and accounted for himself
Admirably but he was up against three billy clubs, Miles'
Head was bloodied, his white shirt stained red and at the
Station house no charges were filed, Miles' view of
America was changed for the rest of his life

SWING, HARD BOP, BOP & BEBOP

The incident must have jinxed Birdland, a little later the
Club filed for bankruptcy and was taken over by Lloyd Price
The rock & roll singer who renamed it the Turntable
The new Birdland is at 44th between Eight and Ninth
Avenues trying to replicate its history with current talents.

HORACE MUNGIN

Minton's Playhouse

The place where bebop was born and proliferated
The home of Monk, Parker, Diz, and Bud Powell
And the free-form jam session, Henry Minton,
Himself a musician and union delegate of Local 802
Protected the musicians from union rules
That penalized them hefty fines for participating
In gigs that didn't produce union dues
Free music for Minton's, Playhouse, a platform to experiment
For the musicians, the patrons and the music benefited

It was in Minton's that Monk got the melody
For the tune "In Walked Bud" a tribute to
The many entrances of his friend and fellow
Pianist Bud Powell, Monk was also a member
Of Minton's house band, that drew other musicians to
The freestyle jam sessions that created the bebop sound
Alto saxophonist Charlie Parker emerged as a leader of
The new bebop movement; Parker's pioneering collaboration
With Dizzy Gillespie, Thelonious Monk and Kenny Clarke,
At sessions at Minton's were breaking innovative ground

Monday night was celebrity night with guest band performers
From the Savoy Ballroom and the Apollo Theater; Jam session
And free food and drinks for all made Minton's the
Place to be for musicians of all stripes on Monday nights

In 1994, after three decades, Minton's closed its door
But reopened in 2006 brand-spanking new
With a new menu of food and a new crop of musicians
And the spirit of Monk, and Diz, and Parker hovering
Over every inch of the new establishment, listening
To every note played there.

The Jazz Mobile

A cultural program that gave work
To musicians in the summer months
When club work was slow;
And brought culture to the black masses
Without money for the Apollo Theater
The Jazz Mobile appeared at locations
Around Harlem on hot sultry evenings
When they could have been
Other things going down

Even top musicians signed up for the program
It got them close to their audience cultivating
A larger following and it provided a payday
And appreciative listeners.

The sessions were informal, but the music
Was tight like these were the most critical
Audiences between a sip of beer and a puff
Of weed.

Absolutely free of charge we listened
To Eddie Harris and Les McCann play
Cold Duck Time for the very first time
On 116 Street and Morningside Avenue
Across from the old Alhambra theater.

HORACE MUNGIN

The Apollo Theater

In the middle of One Hundred and Twenty Fifth Street
In the heart of Harlem, was before 1934 a burlesque hall
For white performers and white theater goers
In white Harlem

The Harlem Renaissance was ending, Harlem
Was changing and the Apollo did too, renamed for the Greek
God and this is when Jazz and entertainment history began
In New York City from the unforgettable appearance
Of 17-year-old Ella Fitzgerald winning the talent
Show with her version of *The Object of my Affections* in 1934
To enshrine Amateur Hour at the Apollo as a celebrated feature
Of Apollo lore and to develop the truest audience in America

Over its history the word Apollo has come to mean to
The rest of the world; Harlem, black, the best in entertainment
Royalty featuring Count Basie, Duke Ellington, and Lady Day
Making careers like James Brown who made more appearances
There than any other entertainer, and when he died
His body was brought back to the Apollo before his funeral
When Paul McCartney appeared at the Apollo
Late in its fame and his, he called it
The Holy Grail and for Tony Bennett
The Apollo is Harlem's Carnegie Hall.

Grant's Tomb

As the quiz does:
Who is in Grant's Tomb?

The answer:
Ulysses Grant, Commanding General of the United States Army
And 18th President of the United States of America

Not tonight baby

Grant is sitting on the hood of a car on Riverside Drive smoking
Weed and listening to Dexter Gordon on the Jazz Mobile

Grant's Tomb in Riverside Park, Harlem, New York
Commanded the largest crowd hot July nights
For yards around the gray stone tomb
The sweet smell of Marijuana marinated
With the sound of cool jazz
Over the hush of the crowd

William Clayton (Pee Wee) Marquette

Master of ceremonies at the Birdland Jazz Club, Pee Wee
Came up from Montgomery, Alabama to find his niche
At the world-famous Birdland Jazz Club on 52nd Street

Pee Wee was the legendary three-foot, nine inches announcer
And Master of Ceremonies whose piercing soprano voice
Became Iconic with 52nd Street, jazz and Birdland, can be
Heard on countless live jazz recordings made at Birdland

A voice so unique, a CD of his introduction of various acts
Was released in 2008, but Pee Wee was notorious for
Mispronouncing the names of acts who didn't tip him
For years Horace Silver was introduced as Whore-Ass Silber
Until he got off of a five spot, Pee Wee once told Bobby Hutcherson
To pack up his shit – he was not needed at Birdland

Pee Wee could be cantankerous and at times mean spirited, Lester Young
A hip coiner of phrases affectionately called Pee Wee Marquette
"Half a motherfucker" while other musicians referred to him as
The Midget, Pee Wee told it all on David Letterman in 1985 and
He sang too.

SWING, HARD BOP, BOP & BEBOP

Symphony Sid Torin

Born Sidney Tarnopoi in the slums of
New York City's Lower East Side in 1909
His family name was shortened to Torin, but
No matter his first name became his last name
His whole life he was known as Symphony Sid
The "Race Music" disc jockey – Symphony because
He once worked at the Symphony Record Store
Sid grew up in Brooklyn, the depression ended his
Bid for college, so he went on the radio in the Bronx
In a show called "Afternoon Swing Session" playing
The biggest hits by Basie, Ellington and Ella, young
People loved the hip talking Jew from Brooklyn

The only white disc jockey to play sepia records
Sid moved from station to station increasing his
Audience, moved to a solid night spot more suitable
For the music, the night shift was called "After-hours
Swing Session" playing the stuff of up and coming
Artists even the new music called bebop, Sid
Became known as the disc jockey most responsible
For the promotion and popularity of the new jazz
Style – Sid loved the style from the very beginning
High-lighted Monk, Diz, Parker – received awards
For his promotion of black artists, in 1948 Sid was
Busted on a weed charge, but he worked until the case
Came up in 1949 and concluded in a mistrial

By the 50's, Sid was the man; the dean of jazz radio
Sid MC-ed jazz concerts, produced and promoted
Concerts; he was so popular musicians wrote several
Tunes dedicated to him, he took Lester Young's "Jumping
With Symphony Sid" as his theme song, but the reefer bust
Had dimmed Sid's luster in New York City and he moved on to
Boston where he hosted both gospel and jazz shows

HORACE MUNGIN

Sid came back to New York City in 1957 to host salsa
And Afro-Cuban Jazz on a socialist owned radio station
Where he was called a traitor to jazz, Sid retired to Florida
In 1973; a heavy smoker, he died of heart disease in 1984
Dubbed the most influential disc jockey in history by the
Rock and Roll Hall of Fame.

SWING, HARD BOP, BOP & BEBOP

Marian McPartland

She was the host of *Marian McPartland's Piano Jazz* on NPR
For 33 years, she was a British American jazz pianist, composer
And writer, after her marriage to trumpeter Jimmy McPartland in
1945, she resided in the United States when not performing around
The world, she was a record producer and a jazz master who threw
Herself into that black American music idiom

Margaret Marian Turner was born March 20, 1918 in Slough
United Kingdom, she played the violin and she displayed an
Early talent for the piano and was found to have perfect pitch
For 11 years she studied at a variety of music schools, before
Concentrating on the piano, at the age of 16, she was stronger
Learning music by listening than by reading notated music
She developed a love for American Jazz notwithstanding her
Classical training at the prestigious Guildhall School of Music
And Drama in London

Marian's talent for improvisation and composition was recognized
When she *won the Wainwright Memorial Scholarship for Composition*
And *the Worshipful Company of Musicians Scholarship*, and the
Chairman School Composition in 1936 and 1937, but to her family's
Dismay she developed a love for the music of Duke Ellington, Fats Waller
Teddy Wilson, Mary Lou Williams and other black American artists

To avoid the draft in World War Two Marian volunteered for the British
Entertainment National Service Association which played for allied
Troops, in 1944 she met Chicago cornetist Jimmy McPartland they
Were married in 1945, after the war, Jimmy and Marian moved to
Chicago to be near his family, Jimmy formed a group that included
Marian and they flourished in Chicago

In 1950, the couple moved to Manhattan and Jimmy encouraged
Marian to form her own trio. She attended the Paris Jazz Festival and
That began her writing career, she covered the festival for Downbeat
As she got booked in more sophisticated clubs, jazz reviewers judgment's
Sharpened Leonard Feathers wrote of her: she's not going to make it,

HORACE MUNGIN

She's English, she's white and she's a woman, Duke Ellington attended one
Of her performances and told her that she played too many notes
Advice she took to heart, she signed her first record deal without Jimmy
In 1951, drummer Joey Morello joined the trio with Bill Crow and that
Unit went strong until the affair between Marian and Morello got back
To his wife and Dave Brubeck hired Morello away from the trio

Marian McPartland was among the 57 jazz musicians who posed for
The famous 1958 picture called *A Great Day in Harlem*, She was one of only
4 of the 57 musicians from the original picture still living when the
Picture was retaken in 2013, Marian and Jimmy divorced in 1972
They remained good friends and remarried in 1991 right before Jimmy's
Death, she started her own record label, she wrote articles for
Downbeat and other jazz magazines and she hosted the longest and
Most decorated cultural program on public radio, in 2010 Marian
McPartland was appointed *Officer of the Order of the British Empire*
She died in 2013 at the age of 95.

SWING, HARD BOP, BOP & BEBOP

Louis Armstrong

Pops had a career that spans the history
Of jazz in its many developments from
Dixieland to bebop, from Boogie Woogie to modern
And all its roots From New Orleans to Paris, France
And its personalities from Sidney Bechet to Miles Davis
Pops was involved in all of the shaping of the music
Louis Daniel Armstrong was born August 4, 1901
In New Orleans, Louisiana, he was nicknamed
Satchmo, Satch, and Pops

A poor boy from a place called the Battlefield
Turn of the century New Orleans, Pop once
Fired a pistol in the air hailing the New Year of 1911
That led to a stint in the Colored Waifs home
Where he learned the cornet; the shot heard round the world

Pop's first wife was a woman of the streets,
Working odd jobs, Pops adopted his deceased cousin's
Mentally ill son while he himself was just a boy and
Supported him for all of his life

Pops played on Riverboats and backed up silent
Movies in theaters orchestra pits
Honing his skills reading music

Pops joined Kid Ory's jazz band featuring King Oliver
He soon replaced Oliver as lead cornet and later without
Malice Oliver got Pops to join his Creole jazz band in Chicago
Where they made their first recording in 1923, and
Even though Pops took Chicago by storm, his Second
Wife pushed him to join Fletcher Henderson's band
In New York City to further exploit his appeal

Playing for the top dance band in New York City

HORACE MUNGIN

Pops created solos that complimented the concept
Of swing music, his influence convinced Henderson
To integrate Pop's swing vocabulary into most of the
Band's arrangements, but Pops soon wary of New York City
Return to Chicago where he assembled a small band
Of his own Louis Armstrong and his Hot Five

The Years 1925 to 1928 with the Hot Five were the
Transforming years; Pops switched from Cornet to trumpet,
Invented scat singing on the recording the Heebie Jeebies
Pops and his Hot Five recorded a record 60 songs in three
Years, by the end of the 1920's Broadway was calling
And now the movies named him Satchmo and
He toured England for the first of many times
Beloved by musicians and audiences, he was called
Too wild, by music critics who gave him racist reviews

Nothing could stop Pop's popularity; he toured all of
Europe becoming so much of a world phenomenon in 1933
That the American government would export to exploit
Only that little problem that his manager got him into
With the Mafia could derail his career and sideline him
Stranded in Europe, he took 1934 off relaxing and resting his lip

On his return to Chicago, Pops hired a new manager who
Had ties to Al Capone and loving Pops he used his
Connections to make Satchmo's trouble disappear, even
Helped to handle the lawsuit brought on by Pop's second
Wife when they split up, within a few months Satchmo
Had assembled a new big band under his new manager
Was recording for Decca Records and married number three

Pops was a great musician, but he was also a showman
A charismatic entertainer who knew what pleased his audience
Wowed by his gravel voice, musical mastery and American spirit
The world gave Pops its love and placed him on a pedestal

The American Government saw Pop's worldwide
Popularity as a useful diplomatic tool and had the State
Department to arrange Friendship tours all over the world
The smiling black face of a man who brought but joy
Would be interpreted as a sign that America was doing
Right by its black citizens when any other inference would
Have been closer to the truth and Pops took flak from
Black leaders for letting them use him in this way

SWING, HARD BOP, BOP & BEBOP

His popularity was hitting new highs in the 1950s, and despite
Breaking down so many barriers and being a hero in the
African-American community Pops began losing his standing
With modern jazz fans and young African-Americans
Bebop, a new form of jazz, had blossomed and the younger
Generation of musicians saw themselves as artists, not entertainers
They saw Pops stage persona and music as old-fashioned
They criticized him in the press, Pops fought back
But for many young jazz fans, he was regarded as an
Out-of-date performer with his best days behind him

In 1957, when Ambassador Satchmo saw the Little Rock
Central High School integration crisis on television, Arkansas
Governor Orval Faubus sent in the National Guard to prevent
The Little Rock Nine African-American students from entering
The public school, Pops saw this as well as white protesters
Hurling invectives at the students, he blew his top to the press,
Telling a reporter that President Dwight D. Eisenhower had "no guts"
For letting Faubus run the country, and stating,
"The way they are treating my people in the South,
The government can go to hell."

This man who had long found his musical voice
Had now found a civic voice suitable to his status
Everybody was not to be satisfied, but now with
His silence broken Pops went on to record
Some of his biggest hits and most memorial recordings

Armstrong died of a heart attack in his sleep on July 6, 1971
A month before his 70th birthday, the house his fourth wife
Purchased in 1941 in Corona, New York is now the Louis
Armstrong Museum and his musical accomplishments are
Recognized around the world – A wonderful world it is.

HORACE MUNGIN

Duke Ellington

An originator of big-band jazz, Edward Kennedy Ellington
Was an American composer, pianist and bandleader who
Composed thousands of scores over his 50-year career, a major
Figure in the history of jazz music, his career spanned more than
Half a century, during which time he composed thousands of songs
For the stage, screen and contemporary songbook, Duke Ellington
Was born April 29, 1899 in Washington, D.C., In the 1920s
Ellington performed in Broadway nightclubs as the bandleader of
A sextet, a group which in time grew to a 10-piece ensemble, Ellington
Sought out musicians with unique playing styles, all the great musicians
Played with Ellington at one time or another; Cootie Williams and Johnny Hodges

Perhaps Ellington's most famous jazz tune was "Take the A Train,"
Which was composed by Billy Strayhorn, Ellington's fame rose to
The top in the 1940s when he composed several masterworks
Including *Concerto for Cootie, Cotton Tail* and *Ko-Ko*. Some
Of his most popular songs included
It Don't Mean a Thing if It Ain't Got That Swing,
Sophisticated Lady,
Prelude to a Kiss,
Solitude,
Satin Doll,
A number of his hits were sung by the impressive Ivie Anderson
A favorite female vocalist of Duke's band

Duke Ellington was raised by two talented musical parents in a
Middle-class neighborhood of Washington D.C., at the age of
Seven, he began studying piano and earned the nickname "Duke"
For his gentlemanly ways, inspired by his job as a soda jerk
He wrote his first composition, *Soda Fountain Rag*, at the age of 15
Despite being awarded an art scholarship to the Pratt Institute
In Brooklyn New York, he followed his passion for ragtime and began
To play professionally at age 17, he was destined to be an artist of another sort

SWING, HARD BOP, BOP & BEBOP

At the age of 19, Ellington married Edna Thompson, who had been
His girlfriend since high school, and soon after their marriage, she gave
Birth to their only child, Mercer Kennedy Ellington, on May 24, 1974
At the age of 75, Duke Ellington died of lung cancer and pneumonia.

HORACE MUNGIN

William James "Count" Basie

In 1958, Count Basie became the first African-American male
Recipient of a Grammy Award, he won nine in his lifetime, a few
Of his songs were inducted into the Grammy Hall of Fame as well
Including "April in Paris" and *Everyday I Have the Blues,* The
Count was a history making musician, composer and band leader

Count Basie was born on August 21, 1904, in Red Bank, New Jersey
His father Harvey was a mellophonist and his mother Lillian was a
Pianist who gave her son his first lessons, after moving to New York
He was further influenced by James P. Johnson and Fats Waller
With Waller teaching Basie organ-playing techniques
He played vaudeville before eventually years later forming his own
Big band and helping to outline the era of swing with hits like
One O'Clock Jump and *Blue Skies*

Count Basie eventually fashioned his own big band, jumping
Into that big band era helping to define the epoch of swing
He got stuck in Kansas in the mid-1920s after his performance
Group disbanded. He went on to join Walter Page's Blue Devils
In 1928, which he found to be a pivotal moment in his career
Because he was introduced to the big-band sound for the first time

He later worked for a few years with a band led by Bennie Moten
Who died in 1935, Basie then formed the *Barons of Rhythm* with
Some of his bandmates from Moten's group, including saxophonist
Lester Young, with vocals by Jimmy Rushing, the band set up shop
To perform at Kansas City's Reno Club

During a radio broadcast of the band's performance, the announcer
Wanted to give Basie's name some glamour, keeping in mind the existence
Of other bandleaders like *Duke* Ellington and *Earl* Hines, so he called the
Pianist *"Count,"* Basie did not realize just how much the name would
Catch on as a form of recognition and respect in the music world
William James Basie was royalty from that moment on – the Count

SWING, HARD BOP, BOP & BEBOP

The Count Basie Orchestra had a huge number of hits that helped to
Define the big-band sound of the 1930s and '40s, some of their notable
Songs included *One O'clock Jump*—the orchestra's signature
Tune which Basie composed himself—and *Jumpin' at the Woodside*
The group became highly distinguished for its soloist's rhythm section
And style of swing, Basie himself was noted for his understated yet
Charismatic style of piano playing and precise impeccable musical
Leadership, he was also leading one of the biggest, most renowned
African-American jazz groups of the day, or any other day
During the 1960s and '70s, Basie recorded with luminaries like
Ella Fitzgerald, Frank Sinatra, Sammy Davis Jr., Jackie Wilson
Dizzy Gillespie and Oscar Peterson, Basie suffered from health
Issues in his later years, and died from cancer in Hollywood,
Florida, on April 26, 1984. He left the world an almost
Unparalleled legacy of musical greatness, having recorded or been
Affiliated with dozens upon dozens of albums during his lifetime.

HORACE MUNGIN

John Hammond

John Hammond was responsible for discovering many of the most
Important figures in 20th century popular music, Hammond was an
American record producer, civil rights activist, and music critic
From the 1930s to the early 1980s, Hammond was instrumental
In sparking or furthering numerous musical careers, he is largely
Responsible for the revival of delta blues artist Robert Johnson's music

Hammond was born in New York City on December 15, 1910
To great privilege, christened John Henry Hammond Jr, his
Mother was Emily Vanderbilt Sloane, his grandfather was
Civil War General John Henry Hammond, his father was a
Brother of Ogden H. Hammond, ambassador to Spain
And uncle to politician Millicent Fenwick, A four-term
Republican female member of the United States House
Of Representatives from New Jersey

Hammond showed interest in music from an early age
At four he began studying the piano, only to switch to
The violin at age eight, he was steered toward classical
Music by his mother, but he was more interested in the music
Sung and played by the servants, many of whom were black
He was known to go down to his basement to listen to the
Upbeat music in the servants' quarters, his youngest sister
Married musician Benny Goodman in 1942

Hammond became interested in social reform at a young age
His mother also promoted social reform as a means to give
Back some of her fortune to the community, she often found
Solace in religion, Hammond shared her desire to help the
Community with his privilege that desire extended into music

Hammond comments that the first jazz music that he heard was in
London in 1923 on a trip with his family he heard a band called
The Georgians, a white Dixieland jazz group, and saw a Negro

SWING, HARD BOP, BOP & BEBOP

Show called *From Dixie to Broadway*, that featured Sidney Bechet
This trip changed the way that he thought about music, upon his
Return to the states, Hammond searched for records by Negro
Musicians but could not find them in the greater Manhattan area
He learned that Negro music was sold in different stores, so he
Began to search for this music in Harlem

At boarding school Hammond succeeded in convincing the headmaster to
Allow him to go into the city every other weekend, Hammond would secretly
Go up to Harlem to hear jazz, during this time he heard Bessie Smith perform
At The Harlem Alhambra, the summer after graduating from Hotchkiss in 1929
He moved to Greenwich Village, where he became involved in a bohemian life and
Worked for an integrated music world, He set up one of the first regular live jazz
Programs, and wrote regularly about the racial divide, I heard no color line
In the music, he is known to have said, Hammond always strived for racial
Integration within the musical scene, for this purpose, he frequently visited
Musicians in Harlem in order to connect with musicians in their own area
While initially, his race proved a problem in connecting with this community
He formed relationships with various musicians that allowed him to overcome
This barrier, his friendship with Benny Carter gave him a status that allowed
Him to enter the black musical community

In 1938, Hammond organized the first *From Spirituals to Swing* concert at
Carnegie Hall, presenting a broad program of blues, jazz and gospel artists
Including Ida Cox, Big Joe Turner, Albert Ammons, Pete Johnson
Meade "Lux" Lewis, Sister Rosetta Tharpe, the Count Basie orchestra
Sidney Bechet, Sonny Terry, James P. Johnson, and Big Bill Broonzy
He coordinated a second *From Spirituals to Swing* concert in 1939

Hammond felt unmoved by the bebop jazz scene of the mid-1940s
Rejoining Columbia Records in the late 1950s, he signed Pete Seeger
And Babatunde Olatunji to the label, and discovered an eighteen-year-old
Gospel singer named Aretha Franklin, in 1961, he heard folk singer
Bob Dylan playing harmonica on a session for Carolyn Hester
He signed him to Columbia and kept him on the label despite the
Protests of executives, who referred to Dylan as "Hammond's folly"
He produced Dylan's early recordings, *Blowin' in the Wind* and
A Hard Rain's a-Gonna Fall

Hammond recognized jazz music to have originated as an
African-American musical genre, When Hammond entered
The jazz community, integration had not yet begun, Hammond
Was able to secure contracts for various musicians, he was an
Appealing producer to these companies because he did not
Want a profit for himself, Hammond broke out of the

HORACE MUNGIN

Traditional role of a producer and became a talent scout
After hearing Billie Holiday

Hammond was instrumental in inspiring or advancing numerous
Musical careers, including those of Bob Dylan, Bruce Springsteen
Benny Goodman, Harry James, Charlie Christian, Billie Holiday
Count Basie, Teddy Wilson, Big Joe Turner, Pete Seeger
Babatunde Olatunji, Aretha Franklin, George Benson, Freddie Green
Leonard Cohen, Arthur Russell, Jim Copp, Asha Puthli
And Stevie Ray Vaughan, in his service as a talent scout, Hammond
Became one of the most influential figures in popular music

Hammond's work with civil rights came from multiple angles
In 1933, he traveled south to attend a trial regarding the Scottsboro case
A case in which two white girls accused nine black boys of raping them
The testimonies of the two girls did not align with the story they told
While all nine boys were convicted, Hammond viewed this trial
As a "catalyst for black activism"

In 1985, Hammond had his first stroke. Although this impaired him
Physically, his wife's death left him in despair, Esme Hammond was
Diagnosed with breast cancer, while treatments worked for some time
She died May 19, 1986, of complications of AIDS, She had contracted
From a blood transfusion, Hammond was distraught and died on
July 10, 1987, after a series of strokes, it is said that he died listening to
The music of Billie Holiday.

SWING, HARD BOP, BOP & BEBOP

Ella Fitzgerald

Ella Fitzgerald was in a class all her own, she created the jazz singer's
Template from the moment she won the amateur contest at the Apollo
Theater in 1934, taking home the $25 first prize money
She would become the *First Lady of Song*, after a troubled childhood
Born April 25, 1917, in Newport News, Virginia, Ella's parents separated
After her birth, she went to Yonkers, New York with her mother, there she
Lived with her mother, her mother's boyfriend, a Portuguese immigrant
Named Joseph Da Silva and a half-sister, the family struggled financially
And Young Ella helped out by becoming a numbers runner and lookout
For a brothel, she wanted to become a dancer since the third grade, but
Her mother died when she was 15, Ella moved in with an aunt in Harlem
And the former solid student became a school truant, she was sent to the
Colored Orphan Asylum in the Bronx for a short while and then to the
New York Training School for Girls, in Hudson, New York, a state
Reformatory, eventually she escaped and in 1934, Ella was homeless and
Trying to make it on her own singing on the streets of Harlem while still
Harboring dreams of becoming an entertainer, she was listening to
Recordings of Louis Armstrong and the Boswell sisters, she wanted to
Sound like Connie Boswell, the lead singer, the chance came at the Apollo
Theater and she sang *The Object of my Affections* sounding just like
Connie Boswell, Her performance at the Apollo Theater set Ella's career
In motion, She met band leader and drummer Chick Webb and soon
Joined his band as a singer, Ella also started performing and recording
With Benny Goodman's Orchestra, Chick Webb died in 1939 and
Ella Fitzgerald took over the band; it was renamed *Ella Fitzgerald and her
Famous Orchestra,* Ella married Ben Kornegay, a convicted drug dealer
And hustler and remained married just long enough for the marriage to be
Annulled in 1941, again on her own, she recorded some hit songs with
Louis Jordan and the Ink Spots, and she made her film debut in a comedy
Western with Bud Abbott and Lou Costello in 1942, her career took off
When the founder of Verve Records started the Jazz at *the Philharmonic
Concert series,* He also became Ella's manager, she went on tour with
Dizzy Gillespie and incorporated scat into her routine, she also fell in love
With Gillespie's bass player Ray Brown, they married and adopted Ella's

HORACE MUNGIN

Half-sister's son, the 50s and 60s brought more critical success, Ella
Gained mainstream popularity, her ability to mimic instrumental sounds
Popularized her vocal improvisations of scatting which became her keynote
Technique, she made some of her most popular albums for Verve Records
Starting with *Ella Fitzgerald Sings the Cole Porter Song Book*, then *Ella
Sings the Duke Ellington Song Book*, and *Ella Sings the Irving Berlin
Song Book* which won her two Grammy's at the very first Grammy Awards
In 1958, from there she went on to make impressive recordings with Count Basie
Louis Armstrong, Frank Sinatra and other greats, she performed in a two
Week engagement with Basie and Sinatra in New York City in 1974, by
The 80s Ella's health was failing, she had heart surgery in 1986 and
She suffered from diabetes, the disease left her blind and in 1994 she
Had both legs amputated, Ella Fitzgerald died in her Beverly Hills
Home on June 15, 1996.

SWING, HARD BOP, BOP & BEBOP

Joe Williams

Joe Williams was born Joseph Goreed; December 12, 1918, in
Cordele, Georgia, his mother and grandmother took him to Chicago
He grew up on the South Side of Chicago, where he attended Austin
Otis Sexton Elementary School and Englewood High School, as a
Teenager, he was a member of a gospel group, the Jubilee Boys
And performed in Chicago churches

He worked as a singer and bouncer in Chicago in the late 1930s
And early 1940s, he began singing professionally as a soloist in
1937, he sometimes sang with big bands, in 1941 he toured with
Coleman Hawkins to Memphis, Tennessee, in 1943 he performed
In Boston with the Lionel Hampton Orchestra, he toured with
Hampton for several years but never achieved a breakthrough success
In October 1950 he was at the Club DeLisa with Red Saunders
Where Count Basie heard him, from 1954 to 1961 he was the singer
For the Count Basie Orchestra *Every Day I Have the Blues*, recorded
In 1955, and *Alright, Okay, You Win*, were among his many successful
Recordings from this period

After leaving the Basie band, Williams had a successful career as a
Soloist at jazz festivals, in clubs and on television, he regularly appeared
With the Basie orchestra, he toured and made recordings with many
Other musicians, including Harry "Sweets" Edison in 1961–62
Junior Mance between 1962 and 1964, George Shearing in 1971
And Cannonball Adderley between 1973 and 1975, he went on a long
Tour from Egypt to India with Clark Terry in 1977, and toured Europe
And the United States with Thad Jones and the Basie Orchestra in 1985
He also worked with his own combos, from between 1970 and 1990

He sometimes worked as an actor, and in 1985 took the role of
Grandpa Al Hanks in Bill Cosby's popular *The Cosby Show*
Williams appeared several times on *Sesame Street* in the 1980s
And early 1990s, Williams often worked in hotels and clubs in
Las Vegas, but also sang at jazz festivals and worked on cruise ships

Williams worked regularly until his death in Las Vegas on March 29, 1999 at the age of 80.

SWING, HARD BOP, BOP & BEBOP

John Birks Gillespie

Gillespie was born in Cheraw, South Carolina
His personality in a word – effervescent
A jig, a shuffle, a grin – salt peanuts, salt peanuts
His humor so prevalent, his pranks surprising
His playfulness so distracting
Fellow musicians called him Dizzy,
Dizzy Gillespie
Dizzy Gillespie's contributions to jazz were huge
The Diz was serious about his music
His band
Played
Salt peanuts, salt peanuts

His beret and horn-rimmed spectacles, his scat singing
His bent horn, pouched cheeks and his light-hearted
Personality were essential in popularizing bebop
Gillespie taught himself how to play the trombone as
Well as the trumpet by the age of twelve, from the night
He heard his idol, Roy Eldridge, play on the radio
He dreamed of becoming a jazz musician
Salt Peanuts, salt Peanuts

Years after Diz and Bird invented bebop Diz
Went treasure hunting in Cuba
Found
Chino Pozo; Latin Jazz, Afro-Cuban Jazz
To broaden the music spectrum in
A most spectacular manner
Not finish yet – salt peanut, salt peanuts
Met Charlie Parker – the Bird and
Along with Thelonious Monk
They blazed a trail to bebop
And Jazz made a ninety-degree turn
To the cool place where

HORACE MUNGIN

Salt peanuts, salt peanuts.

SWING, HARD BOP, BOP & BEBOP

Charles Christopher Parker

Bird had a crying soul, played like he had been hurt
That's what Jay McShann, leader of the first band
Ever to hire Bird said of his sound. It is from the soul
That painters acquire their flair, it is from the soul that
Writers get their grandeur; this is true of musicians too

Charles Christopher Parker was born August 19, 1920
In Kansas City, Kansas, a short while after, he was accredited
With inventing a new musical style called bebop, Bird became
An icon for the hipster subculture; the Beat Generation
Saw him as an uncompromising intellectual, for them
He was more than a mere entertainer, a leading figure in
The development of bebop with his quicken tempo, blazingly
Fast virtuoso, a style so foreign to bandleader Cab Calloway
That he called it Chinese music, centuries later music theorist
Compared Bach's Octave displacement with that being played by Bird

Bird's father was a stage entertainer; his mother was a Native
American, the Parker family moved to Kansas City, Missouri when
Their only son was seven; the young boy took up an instrument
In public school, at this time their new home city was a hot-bed
For African American music; jazz, blues and gospel, Bird
Played in his high school band, His mother gave him his own
Saxophone to cheer him up after his father abandoned the family
Bird was playing with local bands while still in high school
At fifteen he left school to pursue a career in music

The legendary Grammy Award winning saxophonist was
As sloppy with his life as he was flawless with his music
Bird developed a reputation for not showing up for gigs
He was unpredictable and undependable as an employee
But when he showed up, his colleagues enjoyed him as much
As the audiences; He was playing chords changes that had not
Before been articulated, but fables were made of Bird's tardiness
Bird had charming qualities; he spoke with the tact of the upper crust

HORACE MUNGIN

Bird played music everywhere from Kansas City to New England
From New York City to Los Angeles somewhere along the way
He picked up the nickname Yardbird, shorten to Bird to imply
Familiarity and an acquired preference for heroin and liquor, plus
He was always tattered; rumpled suit, dull wrinkled shirt and shabby tie
This was Bird's trademark look, some musicians associated this
Shabby look to Bird's virtuoso and would wrinkle their clothes
Hoping that looking like Bird would help them to play like Bird
Some musicians thought it was the dope that gave Bird his powers
And they follow in that direction and were soon strung-out

Bird went with Jay McShann's band on tour to Chicago and to
New York City, in 1939 he decided to hang around New York
Working during the day and jamming at night, this is when Monk
And Gillespie first became impressed with his unique playing style
Bird went back to Chicago for a short stint then returned to
New York City permanently, he signed on with Earl Hines band
For eight months and then he went with Billy Eckestine, only to
Return with McShann with whom he made his first recordings

In 1945 Bird came into maturity as a musician, he formed his own
Band and played with Gillespie's band on the side, then the two of
Them launched a six-week nightclub tour of Hollywood, together they
Approached the frontier of an entirely new style of jazz, commonly known
As bebop, after the joint tour, Bird stayed on in Los Angeles, performing solo
Until the summer of 1946 when he was hospitalized with a nervous breakdown
On his release he returned to New York City, from 1947 to 1951, Bird
Performed in ensembles and solo at a variety of venues, including clubs
And radio stations, Bird also signed with a few different record labels
From 1945 to 1948, he recorded for Dial, in 1948, he recorded for Savoy
Records before signing with Mercury Records

Throughout his adult life, Bird's problems with heroin addiction and alcoholism
And mental illness caused turbulence in his career and personal relationships
By the time Bird married Rebecca Ruffin in 1936, he had already
Started abusing drugs and alcohol, the couple had two children before
Divorcing in 1939, in 1942, Bird married Geraldine Scott, financial
Stresses created a rift between the couple and Bird turned to heroin
As an escape, he ended up leaving his second wife shortly after they married.

In 1949, Bird made his European debut at the Paris International
Jazz Festival and went on to visit Scandinavia in 1950, meanwhile
Back home in New York, the Birdland Club was being named in his honor
In March of 1955, Parker made his last public performance at Birdland a
Week before his death at the home of Baroness Pannonica de Koenigswarter

SWING, HARD BOP, BOP & BEBOP

Charlie Parker died on a sofa in her Fifth Avenue home; 27 years later
Thelonious Monk died after secluding himself for years in her New Jersey
House, the Medical Examiner list Bird's age at 64 – He was 35, Bird had
A crying soul, played like he had been hurt, said Jay McShann.

HORACE MUNGIN

Lester Young

Known widely as Prez, master of the tenor sax,
Lester Young set a tone all his own
He played relaxed and cool, sophisticated harmonies
Made his bones during his years with the Basie Band
Before he blazed a trail of his own with
Coleman Hawkins, Vic Dickerson, Ben Webster
Gerry Mulligan, Roy Eldridge and then
Lady Day; Billie Holiday

Billy Holiday nicknamed him Prez because
She compared his greatness on his horn with the man
She admired the most – President Franklin Roosevelt
The tag stuck because he was viewed as the leader
By other musicians, He wore a Pork Pie hat
The crowning symbol of his regime

Prez was drafted into the army in 1943
He was assigned to a regular army unit
Not the army band as others were and
Not allowed to play his horn he was
Eventually court-martialed for possession
Of marijuana and he was discharged

After the military Prez's musical creativity
Turned fertile and inexhaustible he recorded
With everyone and appeared everywhere
He even when back to the Basie band

Prez introverted, but hip he invented much
Of the trendy jargon associated with jazz music
He called money "bread" about an upcoming gig
He would ask "how does the bread smell" and he
Described unfortunate situations as an "Ivey Divey"
He was imitated by all the emerging musicians
Of his era lowering the demand for the real thing

SWING, HARD BOP, BOP & BEBOP

He first met Billie Holiday at a jam session
In Harlem in the early 1930s
They hooked up musically and emotionally
In a long-tormented relationship fueled by
Alcohol and drugs; eventually they had
To part ways for each other's survival

By the 50s alcohol had deteriorated Prez's health
He was living in Queens with his third wife
But he couldn't endure being so far away
From the action of 52nd Street so he took a hotel
Room overlooking Birdland where he was
Attended to by younger musicians like
Jackie McLean who brought him soup and cigarettes

Reunited December 8, 1957 for a CBS television special
Prez and Lady Day performed a Holiday tune called
"Fine and Mellow"
Accompanied by Gerry Mulligan, Coleman Hawkins
Roy Eldridge, Ben Webster and Vic Dickerson, they
Gave a performance that was moving and revealing
Billie's singing and Young's solo were brilliant
Unparalleled marvels; extraordinarily emotional
Spectacles, nearly an act of public fornication

Later, in 1959, Prez had to cut short a
European tour because of his worsening health
And died a little after that in his hotel room
Overlooking Birdland, March of 1959; Billie
Declared in the funeral procession that she
Was next and four months later, July 17, 1959
Lady Day perished in Roosevelt Hospital 7
Blocks from the hotel where Prez passed
An Ivey Divey, for sure.

HORACE MUNGIN

Billie Holiday

3,000 people turned out to say goodbye to Lady Day
At her funeral at St. Paul the Apostle Roman Catholic
Church July 21, 1959, among them were all of the heavy
Weights of the music world – Billie Holiday died in
Roosevelt Hospital on 58th Street and Columbus Avenue just
Seven blocks from the hotel where her friend and
Collaborator Lester Young died four months earlier

Born Eleanora Fagan, July 21, 1915, life was hard for Holiday
From the very beginning, her mother was an unmarried
Teenager from the slums of Baltimore, Maryland, the
Young girl was frequently truant and her mother went to
Court over the matter, she was then sent to the House of
Good Shepherd, a facility for troubled Negro girls
In January 1925, only 9 years old at the time, Holiday was
One of the youngest girls there, she was returned to her mother's
Care in August of that year only to return there in 1926
After she had been sexually assaulted, the burdens of her life
Already forming in her voice before she began to sing

In her difficult early life, Holiday found solace in music
Singing along to the records of Bessie Smith and Louis Armstrong
She followed her mother, who had moved to New York City in the
Late 1920s, and worked in a house of prostitution in Harlem for
A time, around 1930, Holiday began singing in local clubs and
Renamed herself "Billie" after the silent film star Billie Dove

Holiday was discovered at the age of 18, by producer John Hammond
While she was performing in a Harlem jazz club, Hammond was
Instrumental in getting Holiday recording work with an up-and-coming
Clarinetist and bandleader Benny Goodman, known for her distinctive
Phrasing and expressive, sometimes melancholy voice, Holiday went on
To record with jazz pianist Teddy Wilson and others in 1935, she made
Several singles, including "What a Little Moonlight Can Do" and

SWING, HARD BOP, BOP & BEBOP

"Miss Brown to You," That same year, Holiday appeared with Duke
Ellington in the film *Symphony in Black*

Around this time, Holiday met and befriended saxophonist Lester Young
Who was part of Count Basie's orchestra on and off for years. He even
Lived with Holiday and her mother Sadie for a while, Young gave Holiday
The nickname "Lady Day" in 1937—the same year she joined Basie's band
In return, she called him "Prez," which was her way of saying that she
Thought he was the greatest, Holiday toured with the Count Basie Orchestra
In 1937, the following year she worked with Artie Shaw and his orchestra
Holiday broke new ground with Shaw, becoming the first female
African American vocalist to work with a white orchestra, Promoters
Objected to Holiday for her race and for her unique vocal style, and she
Ended up leaving the orchestra out of frustration

On her own, Holiday performed at New York's Café Society where
She developed some of her trademark stage persona; wearing gardenias
In her hair and singing with her head tilted back, during this engagement
Holiday also debuted two of her most famous songs, *God Bless the Child*
And *Strange Fruit*, Columbia, her record company at the time, was not
Interested in "Strange Fruit," this was a powerful story about the lynching
Of African Americans in the South, Holiday recorded the song with the
Commodore label instead. "Strange Fruit" is considered to be one of her
Signature ballads, and because of the controversy that surrounded it
Some radio stations banned the record, which helped make it a hit

Holiday sang many songs of stormy relationships, including
T'ain't Nobody's Business If I Do and *My Man*.
These songs reflected her personal romances, which were often destructive
And abusive, Holiday married James Monroe in 1941. Already known to
Drink, Holiday picked up her new husband's habit of smoking opium
The marriage didn't last; they later divorced but Holiday's problems with
Substance abuse continued, her new boyfriend was trumpeter Joe Guy
And with him she started using heroin, after the death of her mother in
October 1945, Holiday began drinking more heavily and escalated her
Drug use to ease her grief, Holiday's drug use caused her a great professional
Setback that same year, she was arrested and convicted for narcotics
Possession in 1947, sentenced to one year and a day of jail time, Holiday
Went to a federal rehabilitation facility in Alderston, West Virginia

Holiday remained a major star in the jazz world and even in popular
Music as well; she appeared with her idol Louis Armstrong in the
1947 film *New Orleans*, albeit playing the role of a maid, because of
Her conviction, she was unable to get the necessary license to play in
Cabarets and clubs, Holiday, however, could still perform at concert

HORACE MUNGIN

Halls and had a sold-out show at the Carnegie Hall not long after her release
With some help from John Levy, a New York club owner, Holiday was later
To get to play in New York's Club Ebony, Levy became her boyfriend and
Manager by the end of the 1940s, joining the long list of the men who took
Advantage of Holiday, her hard living was taking a toll on her voice
Holiday continued to tour and record in the 1950s

Holiday became involved with Louis McKay. The two were arrested
For narcotics in 1956, and they married in Mexico the following year
Like many other men in her life, McKay used Holiday's name and
Money to advance himself, despite all of the trouble she had been
Experiencing with her voice, she managed to give an impressive
Performance on the CBS television broadcast *The Sound of Jazz*
With Ben Webster, Lester Young, and Coleman Hawkins

Holiday gave her final performance in New York City on May 25, 1959
Not long after this event, Holiday was admitted to the hospital for heart
And liver problems, she was so addicted to heroin that she was even
Arrested for possession while in the hospital, On July 17, 1959, Holiday
Died from alcohol and drug-related complications, A who's who of the
Jazz world attended the solemn occasion at St. Paul the Apostle Church
On a sun bright day in San Juan Hill, Manhattan.

Coleman Hawkins

He learned to play the piano at the age of 5 and the cello at 7 and
The tenor saxophone at 9, he went to high school in Chicago
And attended Washburn College in Topeka, Kansas where he
Studied harmony and composition, Coleman Hawkins laid a solid
Foundation for his coming illustrious career as a tenor sax man

Hawkins was born November 21, 1904 in St. Joseph, Missouri
His mother began his musical career with piano lessons in 1909
Hawkins later became known chiefly for his association with
Swing music and the big band era, Hawkins toured the world
With various bands and he played a role in the development of
Bebop, he recorded the first bebop record in 1944 with Dizzy
Gillespie

Hawkins toured New England, the East Coast, and the Midwest
And later the South, his travels took him from The Hague to
Paris to Zurich and beyond, he toured all of Europe as a solo
Performer, in the 1950's he recorded prolifically and the
1960's found him making film and television appearances and
Performing at New York City's Village Gate and Village
Vanguard with his quartet, his last concert was April 20th, 1969
At the North Park Hotel in Chicago, he died a month later from
Pneumonia.

Ben Webster

Ben Webster played violin, piano and sax, born in 1909 in Kansas
City Missouri, He was raised by his mother and a great aunt, Webster
Learned to play the violin in grade school and taught himself to play
Piano well enough to work in silent film theaters in Kansas City and
In Texas, he later acclimated to the tenor saxophone influenced by
Coleman Hawkins and the Kansas City music scene, 1930 Kansas City
Was an incubator for able musicians like Count Basie and Lester Young
Webster honed his craft with numerous jazz and blues bands

By 1940 he was a regular in Duke Ellington's orchestra, Webster's
Style emulated his idol Coleman Hawkins, but he soon found his
Own sound, he was able to play any tempo, so he fit in well with
The ever-improvising Ellington compositions, the up-tempo tunes
Showcased Webster's interpretive ability through his raspy powerful
Solos and his work on ballads with his breathy sensual vibrate set
Webster apart from other jazz saxophone soloist

Ben Webster played with Ellington for 3 years, some say the two had
A falling out, Webster preferred his independence, he wanted to control
His career, the rest of the 40's and the 50's Webster led groups and
Played with the greatest artists of the time including Billie Holiday
Ella Fitzgerald, Carmen McRae and Frank Sinatra

SWING, HARD BOP, BOP & BEBOP

Even with glowing reviews of his jazz albums, Webster found it
Difficult to find steady work in the United States, he played at a nightclub
In London, England and soon found himself booked throughout Europe
In 1969, the elegantly dressed sax man took up permanent residency in
Copenhagen, Denmark, joining expatriate and author James Baldwin and
Other black American Jazz musicians who had immigrated to Europe

Webster drank too much and he grew fat, his health deteriorated
Causing him to have to walk with a cane, Webster suffered a cerebral
Hemorrhage and died in September 20, 1973, his ashes was buried
In a modest grave in Copenhagen.

HORACE MUNGIN

Bud Powell

Born in New York City in 1924, Powell began piano lessons
At age five, by age ten, Bud demonstrated an ability to imitate
Legendary pianists like Art Tatum and Fats Waller, later, Monk
Was another primary influence and became Bud's friend and
Mentor, nurturing the pianist's blossoming talent, memorializing
Powell with a Minton's Playhouse inspired tune "In Walked Bud"

Bud Powell found a level of peace at the piano that few experience
In this world, his unrivaled virtuosic style exuded an emotion and
Power that captivated audiences and musicians alike, one day great
Physical misfortune did interrupt his prolific career and tragically
Shorten his life; Powell pioneered the revolutionary bebop sound
Along with alto saxophonist Charlie Parker, trumpeters Dizzy Gillespie
And Miles Davis, pianist Thelonious Monk, and drummer Max Roach

Powell was engaged in a series of dance bands, his incubation culminating
In his being given the piano chair in the big-time swing orchestra of
Cootie Williams, in late 1943 he was offered the chance to appear at a
Midtown nightclub with the modernist quintet of Oscar Pettiford and
Dizzy Gillespie, but Powell's mother decided he would continue with the
More secure job, with the popular Cootie Williams Band

1945 in Philadelphia, Powell met with a sad twist of fate that dramatically
Altered his life and career, only 20 years old, Powell was brutally beaten
By a policeman, the severity of the policeman's reaction was clearly beyond
What that charge warranted; after the incident, Powell was incoherent and
In great pain, days later, when Powell didn't seem to improve, he went from
Hospital to hospital and eventually was institutionalized for several months
Many who knew him thought he had been experimented on to ruin

Despite his mental instability, Powell was still able to play the piano, he was
Having problems with drinking and with a habit of wandering aimlessly,
At the keyboard, however, Powell needed no help, his meteoric rise to fame
Continued unabated, despite occasional setbacks due to his condition, his

SWING, HARD BOP, BOP & BEBOP

Momentum seemed unstoppable; he became the pianist of choice for tenor
Saxophonist Dexter Gordon, vocalist Sarah Vaughan and other luminaries

Powell was now under the watchful eye of his wife and guardian "Buttercup,"
Because of his mental instability and tendency to wander aimlessly, Powell
Required some supervision, but compositions like "Glass Enclosure" make
Clear that Powell seriously lamented his loss of freedom. Buttercup moved
Bud to Paris, where an adoring French public lavished praise on the pianist
Powell enjoyed his five years in France, but was still unhappy with his lack of
Personal freedom, saxophonist Johnny Griffin, pulled Powell away from Buttercup
After recovering from a bout of illness, Powell began to write music again
Including "In the Mood for a Classic," Powell dedicated to the French people

A 6-week engagement at Powell's old haunt Birdland was arranged that turned
Out to be Powell's triumphant return to New York, Bud garnered more accolades
From the press than he had in his entire career, his daughter Celia and her mother
Mary Francis Funderburk were among the electrified Birdland audience first night
Back in New York, Bud lapsed back into his destructive tendencies, most notably
Alcohol dependency, the following year was a downward spiral; Powell died on
July 1, 1966 of cirrhosis of the liver, he was just 41.

HORACE MUNGIN

King Pleasure

Born as Clarence Beeks in Oakdale, Tennessee, March 24, 1922
King Pleasure was a jazz vocalist and an early master of vocalese
Where a singer sings words to a famous instrumental solo
He moved to New York City in the mid-1940's, worked as
A bartender and became a fan of bebop music and then
King Pleasure achieved popularity by singing the Eddie Jefferson
Vocalese classic *Moody's Mood For Love*, based on a 1949 James
Moody saxophone solo to *I'm In The Mood For Love*

King Pleasure and Betty Carter also recorded a famous vocalese version
Of "Red Top", a jazz classic penned by Kansas City's Ben Kynard and
Recorded by Gene Ammons, other notable recordings include a clairvoyant
Lamented version of "Parker's Mood", the year before Charlie Parker died in
1955, and Pleasure's take on Gene Ammons's *Hittin' The Jug*

Pleasure has been cited as a significant influence by Van Morrison
Especially on his album *Astral Weeks*

Pleasure died on March 21, 1982, 3 days before his 60th birthday.

SWING, HARD BOP, BOP & BEBOP

Miles Davis

Everything there is was cool about Miles Davis
His name, his manner, his intense eyes, he was
Born into a middle class black family in a 1920's
America – how likely is that – the cat started
Life from a cool perch, his father was a dental
Surgeon; mother a music teacher in East St. Louis
Illinois, May 26, 1926, the birth of the cool – Miles
Dewey Davis III – his parents owned a 200-acre estate
Near Pine Bluff, Arkansas with a profitable pig farm
From where Miles and his siblings went horseback riding
Hunted and fished, Mile became interested in music
Really young, started trumpet lessons at 12, played
Local gigs and out-of-town gigs by 16, at 17, Miles
Joined Eddie Ranle's Blue Devils, after high school
Graduation Miles got to sit in with Billy Eckstine's
Band in East St. Louis where he met the architects of
The emerging bebop, Dizzy Gillespie and Charlie Parker

It was peculiar that Miles was so taken with the bebop
Architects, their styles were so different from his
Birth of the Cool, but bebop was the sound of the day
And young Miles was compelled to follow it, he did by
Leaving the Midwest to attend the Juilliard School of
Music and Arts in September 1944, soon after his arrival
In Manhattan, he was playing in clubs with Charlie Parker
And by 1945 he had abandoned his academic studies for
A full-time career as a jazz musician, and making his first
Recordings as a sideman with Benny Carter's band before
Going back to Eckstine, Miles alternated between Eckstine
And Parker's bands until 1947 when he led his own group

In 1949, Miles put together a nine-piece band that employed
An unusual horn section, besides Miles on trumpet, the band also
Featured an alto saxophone, a baritone saxophone, a trombone
A French horn, and a tuba, the group produced 12 tracks that

HORACE MUNGIN

Attracted little attention at first, the band's relaxed sound however
Affected the musicians who played it, and it had a profound
Influence on the development of the cool jazz style on the
West Coast, in February 1957, Capitol finally issued the tracks
Together on an LP called Birth of the Cool
Birth of the cool, but the trumpeter's progress was hampered
An addiction to heroin that plagued him in the early 1950s
He managed to kick his habit by the middle of the decade
And he made a strong impression playing "*Round Midnight*"
At the Newport Jazz Festival in July 1955, a performance that
Led major-label Columbia to sign him, the prestigious contract
Allowed him to put together a permanent band and he organized
A quintet featuring saxophonist John Coltrane, pianist Red Garland
Bassist Paul Chambers and drummer Philly Joe Jones, who began
Recording his Columbia debut, *'Round About Midnight*, in October

His next band recording, *"Kind of Blue,"* in March and April 1959
Was an album that became a landmark in modern jazz and the most
Popular album of the trumpeter's career, eventually selling over
Two million copies, a phenomenal success for a jazz record

Birth of the Cool had made its mark replacing bebop for a large
Segment of jazz fans, Miles Davis played the trumpet in a lyrical
Introspective, and melodic style, often employing a stemless Harmon
Mute to make his sound more personal and intimate, but if his approach
To his instrument was constant, his approach to jazz was dazzlingly
Changeable, Doo-Bop, his last studio album, appeared in 1992 was
A collaboration with rapper Easy Mo Bee, and it won a Grammy
For Best Rhythm & Blues Instrumental Performance, with the track
"Fantasy" nominated for Best Jazz Instrumental Solo.

Miles died of pneumonia, respiratory failure, and stroke months before
The release of Doo-Bop.

SWING, HARD BOP, BOP & BEBOP

Art Blakey

Born October 11, 1919 in Pittsburgh Pennsylvania, Blakey's mother
Died shortly after his birth, his father had already abandoned the family
Blakey and his siblings were raised by a friend of his mother, Blakey
Learned to carry adult responsibilities as a child, this later endowed
Him with the leadership ability to organize and manage endeavors
Even the intangibilities of sound and instruments making those sounds

Blakey took piano lessons as a small child, he married and had children
While still in his early teens then he took up the drums and excelled
Quickly, he played with Mary Lou Williams in 1942, then graduated to
Fletcher Henderson's orchestra, from there, he stayed with the band of
Billy Eckstine until 1947, he headed his own band – the 17 Messengers

Blakey traveled to Africa in 1949, searching, he studied Islam and
Received the name Abdullah Ibn Buhaina. When he returned to the
States, he formed a quintet with pianist Horace Silver – the Jazz
Messengers; with Hank Mobley on Sax, Kenny Dorham on trumpet
And Doug Watson on bass, Blakey simultaneously nurtured a
Relationship with the Blue Note label that resulted in some great
Recordings over several years including *Ugetsu* recorded at Birdland

The Jazz Messengers had an evolving membership and a developing
Roster size and developed into a kind of music academy, Established
Musicians left as new ones took their place, Blakey mentored them all
Benny Golson, Donald Byrd, Lee Morgan, Wayne Shorter, Cedar Walton
Charles Fambrough, Terence Blanchard, Branford and Wynton Marsalis

HORACE MUNGIN

Art Blakey earned an instrumental Grammy with the Messengers for the 1984 album *New York Scene*, his classic single *Morning'* was inducted Into the Grammy Hall of Fame in 1998 and the album by the same name Was inducted three years later

Art Blakey died in New York City on October 16, 1990 of lung cancer He was 71 years old.

Horace Silver

The core feeling about the music of Horace Silver was his down
To earth, bluesy tones, Silver was a soul-man, his early piano
Influences included the styles of boogie-woogie and the blues
Silver was born on September 2, 1928, in Norwalk, Connecticut
His mother, Gertrude, was from Connecticut; his father
John Tavares Silver, was born on the island of Maio, Cape Verde
His father taught him the folk music of Cape Verde, Silver began
Playing the piano in his childhood and had classical music lessons

From ninth grade Silver played Lester Young-influenced tenor
Saxophone in the Norwalk High School band and orchestra
Silver played gigs locally on both piano and tenor saxophone
While still at school, he was rejected for military service by a draft board
Examination that concluded that he had an excessively curved spine
Which also curtailed his saxophone playing, in 1946 he moved to
Hartford, Connecticut to take up a regular job as pianist in a nightclub

In 1950, when his trio backed saxophonist Stan Getz at a club in Hartford
Getz liked Silver's band and recruited them to tour with him, Getz also gave
Silver his recording debut, in December 1950, for the *Stan Getz Quartet* album
After a year, Silver moved to New York City, working as a freelancer, he quickly
Having built a reputation, based on his compositions and bluesy playing, Silver was also
Busy recording as a sideman, in 1953, he was pianist on sessions led by Sonny Stitt
Howard McGhee, and Al Cohn, and, the following year, he played on albums by
Art Farmer, Miles Davis, Milt Jackson and others, Silver won the *Down Beat* critics'
New Star award for piano players in 1954, and appeared at the first Newport Jazz
Festival, substituting for John Lewis in the Modern Jazz Quartet

Silver and Blakey co-founded the Jazz Messengers, a cooperatively-run group
That initially recorded under various leaders and names, their first two studio
Recordings, with Hank Mobley on tenor saxophone, Kenny Dorham on trumpet
And Doug Watkins on bass, were made in late 1954 and early 1955 and were

HORACE MUNGIN

Released as two 10-inch albums under Silver's name, this album contained Silver's First hit, "The Preacher," which was pivotal in the development and defining of hard bop which combined elements of blues, gospel, and R&B, with bebop-based Harmony and rhythm, the new, funky hard bop was commercially popular

Silver's final recordings with the Jazz Messengers were in May 1956, he left Blakey after one and a half years, soon after leaving, Silver formed his own Long-term quintet, after receiving offers of work from club owners who had Heard his albums, the first line-up was Mobley (tenor saxophone), Art Farmer (Trumpet), Watkins (bass), and Louis Hayes (drums), the quintet, with various Line-ups, continued to record, helping Silver to build his reputation, he wrote Almost all of the material they played, and, in concert, he "won over the Crowd" through his affable personality, he crouched over the piano as the sweat Poured out, with his forelock brushing the keys and his feet pounding, Silver's Compositions include, *Song for My Father, Sister Sadie, Doodlin, The Preacher The Cape Verdi Blues, The Tokyo Blues, Finger Poppin'* and dozens more

Silver received a National Endowment for the Arts Jazz Masters award in 1995 And in the following year was added to *Down Beat*'s Jazz Hall of Fame, in 2006, *Let's Get to the Nitty Gritty: The Autobiography of Horace Silver*, was published By the University of California Press, Horace Silver died in New York on June 18, 2014 at the age of 85.

SWING, HARD BOP, BOP & BEBOP

Charlie Mingus

Charlie Mingus was diagnosed with amyotrophic lateral sclerosis
(Lou Gehrig's disease) in 1977, his music has been described as
Ambitious, earthy, radical and traditional, Mingus was influenced
By African American gospel and the music of composer, pianist
Duke Ellington, but he was also inspired by modern classical music

Mingus was born April 22, 1922 in Nogales, Arizona, His father
Was of African and Swedish ancestry; his mother was Chinese
And African American, She died shortly after Mingus's birth
Mingus and his two older sisters were raised by a stepmother in
Los Angeles, Mingus felt the lash of racial prejudices intently
Lots of jazz musicians did, but Mingus incorporated what he felt
Into his music, Mingus started out playing the trombone, he
Switch to cello and then to the bass when he was a teenager

Mingus played professionally with Louis Armstrong and Kid Ory
In the early 40's, he wrote and played with Lionel Hampton's band
And toured with Red Norvo's trio before he settled in New York
City in 1951 where he worked as a sideman with Charlie Parker
Bud Powell and Miles Davis

Mingus recorded more than 100 albums over the course of his career
One of his most popular short compositions is "Goodbye, Pork Pie Hat,"
A tribute to jazz saxophonist Lester Young, in the early 1960s, Mingus
Performed regularly as a bandleader at clubs in New York and festivals
Around the country, he became known for erratic behavior both on and
Off the stage, and for fits of temper that sometimes ended in violence
Against fellow musicians or audience members, by the end of the decade
Mingus was suffering from mental illness, from 1967 to 1972, stricken
With severe depression, he rarely appeared in public. However, he
Gradually recovered enough to make a comeback, Mingus was awarded
A Guggenheim Fellowship for composition in 1971, and he renewed his
Activities as a recording artist and performer the following year

HORACE MUNGIN

He was with his wife, Susan, in Cuernavaca, Mexico, when he died of a
Heart attack on January 5, 1979, just months earlier, Mingus had
Completed work on his final studio project, Mingus—a collaboration
With singer-songwriter Joni Mitchell that was released in June 1979.

SWING, HARD BOP, BOP & BEBOP

Oscar Peterson

Oscar Emmanuel Peterson, was born August 15, 1925 in Montreal, Quebec, Canada
A Canadian jazz pianist and composer, he was called the "Maharaja of the keyboard"
By Duke Ellington, he released over 200 recordings, won eight Grammy Awards
And received numerous other awards and honors, he is considered one of the
Greatest jazz pianists ever, and played thousands of concerts worldwide in a career
Lasting more than 60 years, Peterson was born to immigrants from the West Indies
His father, an amateur trumpeter and pianist, was one of his first music teachers
Peterson grew up in the neighborhood of Little Burgundy in Montreal, Quebec
It was in this predominantly black neighborhood that he found himself surrounded
By the jazz culture, Peterson's distinctive playing formed during the mid-to-late
1940's and fell somewhere between swing and bop

At nine Peterson played piano with control that impressed professional musicians
For many years his piano studies included four to six hours of daily practice,
Only in his later years did he decrease his practice to just one or two hours daily
In 1940, at fourteen years of age, Peterson won the national music competition
Organized by the Canadian Broadcasting Corporation, after that victory, he dropped
Out of the High School of Montreal, where he played in a band with Maynard
Ferguson, and became a professional pianist working for a weekly radio show and
Playing at hotels and music halls

Impresario Norman Granz heard Peterson in 1949 and presented him as a surprise
Guest at a Jazz at the Philharmonic concert, Granz recorded Peterson in 1950 on
A series of duets with either Ray Brown or Major Holley on bass; his version of
"*Tenderly*" became a hit, Peterson's talents were quite obvious, and he became
A household name in 1952 when he formed a trio with guitarist Barney Kessel
And Brown, there were many versions of the trio until the 1970's

Underrated as a composer, Peterson wrote and recorded the impressive
"*Canadiana Suite*" in 1964, Peterson developed a reputation as a technically
Brilliant and melodically inventive jazz pianist and became a regular on
Canadian radio from the 1940's, some of Peterson's best playing was as an
Understated accompanist to singer Ella Fitzgerald and trumpeter Roy Eldridge
Oscar Peterson at the Stratford Shakespearean Festival is widely regarded as

HORACE MUNGIN

The landmark album in Peterson's career

Peterson had arthritis since his youth, later years he could hardly button his shirt
His weight increased to 276 hindering his mobility, he had hip replacement
Surgery in the early 1990's, he performed through failing health for decades
Peterson's health declined rapidly in 2007, he had to cancel his performance at
The 2007 Toronto Jazz Festival and his attendance at a June 8, 2007, Carnegie Hall
All-star performance in his honor, owing to illness, On December 23, 2007
Peterson died of kidney failure at his home in Mississauga, Ontario.

Gerry Mulligan

Gerry Mulligan was born April 6, 1927 in Queens Village, New York
Mulligan's father was an engineer who moved frequently to find work
Mulligan was less than a year old when the family moved to Marion, Ohio
Where his father accepted a job with the Marion Power Shovel Company
Mulligan's mother hired an African-American nanny to help care for her
Four sons, who became especially fond of the youngest Mulligan
Mulligan began spending time at the nanny's house and was especially
Amused by her player piano which had rolls by numerous musicians
Including Fats Waller, Black musicians often came through town, and because
Many motels would not take them; they often had to stay at homes within
The black community, occasionally meeting such musicians at the
Nanny's home, became Mulligan's baptism into the world of black music

Mulligan started on the piano before learning clarinet and the various
Saxophones, His initial reputation was as an arranger, he moved to
New York City in 1946 and joined Gene Krupa's Orchestra as a staff
Arranger, the rare times he played with Krupa's band he played alto
Gerry Mulligan's first notable recorded work on baritone was with
Miles Davis' Birth of the Cool, but once again his arrangements
Were more significant than his short solos, when he traveled to Los Angeles
He wrote some arrangements and worked at the Lighthouse Cafe and then
Gained a regular Monday night engagement at the Haig, around this time
Mulligan realized that he enjoyed the extra freedom of soloing without
A pianist, he jammed with trumpeter Chet Baker and soon their magical
Rapport was featured in his pianoless quartet, the group caught on quickly
In 1952 and made both Mulligan and Baker into stars

A drug bust put Mulligan out of action and ended that quartet but, he was
Released from jail in 1954, Mulligan began a new musical partnership with
Valve trombonist Bob Brookmeyer that was just as successful, trumpeter
Jon Eardley and Zoot Sims on tenor occasionally made the group a sextet
And in 1958 trumpeter Art Farmer was featured in Mulligan's Quartet
During 1957-60 he recorded separate albums with Thelonious Monk
Paul Desmond, Stan Getz, Ben Webster and Johnny Hodges, Mulligan

HORACE MUNGIN

Played on the classic Sound of Jazz television special in 1958 and appeared In the movies *I Want to Live* and *The Subterraneans, in 1982* Mulligan Played soprano saxophone in a New York Philharmonic performance of *Ravel's Bolero,* Mulligan worked to build and promote a repertoire of Baritone saxophone music for orchestra, in 1987, Mulligan performed Beside *Entente* with the Israel Philharmonic in Tel Aviv with Zubin Mehta conducting, Mulligan died in Darien, Connecticut, on January 20 1996, at the age of 68, following complications from knee surgery, His Widow Franca, said he had also been suffering from liver cancer.

SWING, HARD BOP, BOP & BEBOP

Julian Edwin (Cannonball) Adderley

Adderley had such a voracious appetite that his high school
Colleagues gave him the nickname Cannibal which eventually
Evolved to Cannonball, born Julian Edwin Adderley in Tampa
Florida on September 15, 1928, Adderley became the band
Director at Dillard's High School in Fort Lauderdale after he
Finished his music studies at Florida A&M – a legend

He and his brother cornetist Nat played with Ray Charles's
Band while Charles lived in Tallahassee, Cannonball moved
To New York City in 1955, one night in 1955 he brought his
Saxophone with him to the Café Bohemia, asked to sit in with
Oscar Pettiford in place of his band's regular saxophonist the
Talk on the New York jazz scene after Adderley's
Performance proclaimed him the heir to Charlie Parker

Adderley formed his own group with his brother Nat after signing
Onto the Savoy jazz label in 1957, he was noticed by Miles Davis
It was his blues-rooted alto saxophone that Davis asked him to
Play with his group, he joined the Davis band in October 1957
Three months prior to the return of John Coltrane to the group
Some of Davis's finest trumpet work is found on Adderley's first
Solo album *Somethin' Else,* with Art Blakey and Hank Jones

Adderley's *Mercy, Mercy, Mercy* became a crossover hit
On the pop Charts in 1966, Adderley was part of two landmark
Davis albums, *Milestones* (1958) and *Kind of Blue* (1959)
Adderley later collaborated with song stylist Nancy Wilson
On an esteemed 1962 record

HORACE MUNGIN

Adderley had a cerebral hemorrhage and four weeks later
On August 8, 1975, he died at St. Mary Methodist
Medical Center in Gary, Indiana. He was 46 years old
He was buried in the Southside Cemetery, Tallahassee.

John Coltrane

John Coltrane championed many younger free jazz musicians such as
Archie Shepp, and under his influence Impulse! became a leading
Free jazz record label, John William Coltrane, also known as "Trane"
Was born September 23, 1926, in Hamlet, North Carolina, He grew up
In High Point, North Carolina, attending William Penn High School

Beginning in December 1938 Coltrane's aunt, grandparents, and father
All died within a few months of one another, leaving John to be raised
By his mother and a close cousin, in June 1943 he moved to Philadelphia
In September of that year his mother bought him his first alto saxophone
Coltrane played the clarinet and the alto horn in a community band before
Taking up the alto saxophone during high school, he had his first professional
gigs in early to mid-1945 with a cocktail lounge trio, with piano and guitar

Coltrane worked in the bebop and hard bop idioms early in his career
Coltrane was later at the forefront of free jazz, he led fifty recording
Sessions during his career, and appeared as a sideman on many albums
By other musicians, including trumpeter Miles Davis and pianist
Thelonious Monk

HORACE MUNGIN

As his career progressed, Coltrane and his music took on an increasingly spiritual
Dimension, Coltrane influenced innumerable musicians, and remains one of
The most significant saxophonists in music history, he received many Posthumous
Awards and recognitions, including canonization by the African Orthodox Church
As Saint John William Coltrane and a special Pulitzer Prize in 2007, his second
Wife was pianist Alice Coltrane and their son, Ravi Coltrane is also a saxophonist

Coltrane's death surprised many in the musical community who were not aware
Of his condition, Miles Davis said that "Coltrane's death shocked everyone
Took everyone by surprise, Coltrane died of liver cancer at Huntington Hospital
On Long Island on July 17, 1967, at the age of 40, his funeral was held four days
Later at St. Peter's Lutheran Church in New York City, the service was opened
By the Albert Ayler Quartet and closed by the Ornette Coleman Quartet, Coltrane
Is buried at Pine Lawn Cemetery in Farmingdale, New York.

Coltrane Talks to God

Let me introduce the players:
Miles Davis on trumpet
John Coltrane on saxophone
Wynton Kelly on piano
Paul Chambers on bass and
Billy Cobb on drums

Teo

Da dum tum/da dum tum/da dum tum

After a few bars of a thumping bass introduction
The rhythm section joins in for a few bars more
Before Miles begins the sacrament with a calm call
Evoking flourishes from the ensemble that slowly evolve
Into a delightful bounce of notes that dance with
Themselves enchanted and charmed
Each by the other

Energy, the flow of energy and the spirit are summoned
Ultimate realities the All of All that is - the sameness
All distinctions are relative comparisons
We now will hear the shapes and the forms
Which cannot be expressed in words
The only contrast to what is unknown
Nonetheless instinctively adhered to

Miles blows a series of sharp notes
That jolt the atmosphere and repeats
Again and again in slight variations
Developing into the resolve of the hymn
Of preparation for the sermon – all the while
The rhythm section is keeping up a driving orderliness
While Miles elaborates an unobtrusive passion like
The energy that amassed before the big bang
And rolls out the expansion of the universe
For now this orderliness exists to contain
Within its perimeter what's to come

A piano interlude builds to reaffirm

HORACE MUNGIN

The primacy of orderliness before
Coltrane burst into consciousness
And then it happens:
Coltrane enters like cleansing rain
Thunder and lightning Illuminating
Abandoned streets on a dark Harlem night
A gathering for all concerned coalitions
Echoes of the turmoil of the times coalesce
The emotion builds and becomes intricate, convoluted
And twists over and over again and changes into
Repeated screams – dark and chaotic
Turbulent images bubble within framed orderliness
Coltrane makes repeated calls gathering all complexities
Then he beseeches in a new language of shapes and forms
Chaotic precision an oxymoron regarding quantum mechanics
The Theory of Everything –
Particles of subatomic sounds beseeching
Beseeching earnestly beseeching

This has been a voyage to awareness

Coltrane is disengaging from the unpredictable
Turbulence of subatomic particles
And glides up to earthly realities where
Miles can handle the transfer though
He is exhausted from the energy spent
Translating the logic of Coltrane's sermon
In a few tones he regains the confidence of his
Own instincts which are born anew from
The Coltrane recital – we are all one now
Miles sounds his last note -
Understanding is at the core of every quest
The rhythm section alone closed the curtains.

SWING, HARD BOP, BOP & BEBOP

Thelonious Monk

Thelonious Sphere Monk who often referred to himself as
"The Onlyist Monk" was born October 10, 1917, in Rocky Mount
North Carolina, in 1922, the family moved to 243 West 63rd Street
In Manhattan, New York City; the neighborhood was known as
San Juan Hill because of the many African-American veterans of
The Spanish–American War who lived there, urban renewal displaced
The long-time residents of the community, who saw their beloved
Neighborhood replaced by the Amsterdam Housing Projects and
Lincoln Center for the Performing Arts, Monk started playing the
Piano at the age of six and was largely self-taught, he attended
Stuyvesant High School, a public school for gifted students

In his early teens, Monk toured with an evangelist, playing the
Church organ, and in his late teens he began to find work playing
Jazz, in the early to mid-1940's, he was the house pianist at Minton's
Playhouse, Much of Monk's style was developed during his time at
Minton's when he participated in after-hours cutting contests
Monk's musical work at Minton's was crucial in the formulation of bebop
Monk's style at this time was later described as "hard-swinging," with
The addition of runs in the style of Art Tatum, Monk's stated influences
Included Duke Ellington, James P. Johnson, and other early stride pianists
In the documentary *Thelonious Monk: Straight, No Chaser*, it is stated that
Monk lived in the same neighborhood in New York City as Johnson and
Knew him as a teenager

Mary Lou Williams, who mentored Monk and his contemporaries, spoke of
Monk's rich inventiveness in this period, and how such invention was vital
For musicians, since at the time it was common for fellow musicians to
Incorporate overheard musical ideas into their own works without giving
Due credit, so the boppers worked out a music that was hard to steal
They tried though; they could be seen in Minton's busily writing on
Their shirt cuffs or scribbling on the tablecloth, and even some home guys

HORACE MUNGIN

Did not give Monk the credit he had coming, they even stole his idea of
The beret and bop glasses

In 1944 Monk made his first studio recordings with the Coleman Hawkins
Quartet, Hawkins was one of the earliest established jazz musicians to promote
Monk, and the pianist later returned the favor by inviting Hawkins to join him
On a 1957 session with John Coltrane, Monk married Nellie Smith and in 1949
The couple had a son, T. S. Monk (called Toot), who became a jazz drummer,
A daughter, Barbara (affectionately known as Boo-Boo), was born in 1953 and
Died of cancer in 1984

After intermittent recording sessions for Blue Note from 1947 to 1952
Monk was under contract to Prestige Records for the following two years
With Prestige, he cut several highly significant, but at the time under-recognized
Albums, including collaborations with the saxophonist Sonny Rollins and the
Drummers Art Blakey and Max Roach, in 1954, Monk paid his first visit to Paris
As well as performing at concerts, he recorded a solo piano session for French
Radio, backstage, Mary Lou Williams introduced him to Baroness Pannonica
"Nica" de Koenigswarter, a member of the Rothschild family and a patroness of
Several New York City jazz musicians, she was a close friend for the rest of
Monk's life, including taking responsibility for him when she and Monk were
Charged with marijuana possession

Monk relaunched his New York career with a landmark six-month residency
At the Five Spot Cafe in the East Village neighborhood of New York beginning
In June 1957, leading a quartet with John Coltrane on tenor saxophone
Wilbur Ware on bass, and Shadow Wilson on drums, The Five Spot residency
Ended Christmas 1957; Coltrane left to rejoin Davis' group, and the band was
Effectively disbanded, Monk did not form another long-term band until June
1958 when he began a second residency at the Five Spot, again with a quartet
This time with Charlie Rouse on tenor, Ahmed Abdul-Malik on bass, and Roy
Haynes on drums

Working with producer Teo Macero on his debut for Columbia, the sessions in
The first week of November had a lineup that had been with him for two years
Tenor saxophonist Rouse, who worked with Monk from 1959 to 1970, bassist
John Ore, and drummer Frankie Dunlop, *Monk's Dream*, his first Columbia album
Was released in 1963, *Monk's Dream* became the best-selling LP of his lifetime
On February 28, 1964, he appeared on the cover of *Time* magazine, being featured
In the article "*The Loneliest Monk*." Monk continued to record studio albums
Including *Criss Cross*, also in 1963, and *Underground*, in 1968

Monk had disappeared from the scene by the mid-1970s and made only a small
Number of appearances during the final decade of his life, Monk was hospitalized

SWING, HARD BOP, BOP & BEBOP

On several occasions owing to an unspecified mental illness that worsened, at least
One of Monk's psychiatrists failed to find evidence of manic depression
Bipolar disorder or schizophrenia, another physician maintains that Monk was
Misdiagnosed and prescribed drugs during his hospital stay that may have
Caused brain damage, his health declined, Monk's last six years were spent as a
Guest in the Weehawken, New Jersey, home of his long-standing patron and friend
Pannonica de Koenigswarter, who had also nursed Parker during his final illness
She proved to be a steadfast presence, as did his own wife Nellie, especially as his
Life descended into further isolation, Monk did not play the piano during this time
Even though one was present in his room, and he spoke to few visitors, he died of
A stroke on February 17, 1982.

HORACE MUNGIN

Thelonious Monk on Amsterdam Avenue

Sounds of the movement of life fill the unseen
Spaces of New York City as elsewhere but listen here
To New York City's Amsterdam Avenue
On Sixty-Fourth Street

Life resonates differently during the recurring
Cycles of summer and winter/day and night
Sounds are dissimilar in the morning from noon
To evening and 'round midnight
Echoes of the rhythms of life set to an uneven tempo
This cacophony of sounds emanating
From the energy of our animation

The street is filled with the sounds of traffic
Automobile engines make a sundry noise
Horns shriek an irregular cadence
Hundreds of tires peel from the pavement over
And over again and the sound dims in the distance
Tires sink into potholes making sounds like
The beat of a bass drum keeping time
An ice cream truck bell rings a metallic allure
A voice calls out from across the street
Like Charlie Rouse on Boo Boo's birthday

The traffic-light is a maestro who orchestrates but
With two commands
Red and Green/Stop and Go

To hear all these sounds is to be in the moment
To value these sounds is to be consciously
Linked to the cosmos
To transfer them into another genre
Deepens their aesthetics
Acquiring this ability takes a prodigious artist
With a blank music sheet versed in a great art
Monk stomp his foot to the pavement
And throw out his arms as antennas
To take in the sounds

SWING, HARD BOP, BOP & BEBOP

He recognizes the hesitation between the lyrical clamors
And it's expected monotonous cadenced
He smiles at the missing beat and he owns it
He hears the nimble tinkle of sounds that make harmony
With their huskier relatives after bypassing
The notes that are in their natural progression
And he adopts it and adapts it into a technique
Of off beats and silence and decisive hesitancy
He combines this new discovery with hip idioms he
Had mastered from the past in Straight no Chaser
He finds his route maneuvering in heavy traffic

Monk pulls in his antennas
Regains a walking stance
Covers his delicate fingers with gray gloves
And reaching Sixty-Fourth Street
He turns the corner

Now he composes with an original ear a billboard
Of pioneering musical enchantments shaped from the
Sounds of life in the unseen spaces on Amsterdam Avenue.

HORACE MUNGIN

Baroness Pannonica de Koenigswarter

She was born in London on Dec. 10, 1913, her full name was
Kathleen Annie Pannonica Rothschild, She was the granddaughter
Of Nathan Mayer, the first Lord Rothschild, and the great-granddaughter
Of Mayer Amschel, the Rothschild patriarch who, from the Frankfurt
Ghetto, orchestrated his family's rise, her father was Nathaniel Charles
Rothschild, a partner in the family bank, a Rothschild heiress, she
Offered her home to countless jazzmen as a place to work and even live
While quietly paying their bills when they couldn't find work

She was likened to the great royal patrons of Mozart or Wagner's day
She never put the spotlight on herself, but she really loved jazz music and
Jazz musicians, she chauffeured them to gigs around New York, toured
With them as a kind of racial chaperon, and was even known to confront
Anyone she felt was taking advantage of her friends because they were black
In 1955 Charlie Parker died on a sofa in her Fifth Avenue home; 27 years later
Thelonious Monk died after secluding himself for years in her New Jersey house
Both deaths made the baroness an immediate target of tabloid headlines and a
Long-term subject for scurrilous gossip

Nica Rothschild, as she was known, became an aviation enthusiast
And an accomplished pilot, at 21 she met a kindred spirit
Baron Jules de Koenigswarter, 31, he was a French mining engineer
Banker and pilot and like Nica, he was Jewish, the baron quickly
Proposed after just three months; her response was a flight to New York
They were married at City Hall in October 1935; the couple took up
Residence in a 17th-century chateau not far from Normandy, when
The Nazis invaded France, the baron, a lieutenant in the reserves
Was called up, he left the baroness a map, with instructions to take
The children and escape to her family in England

Next the baroness moved their two children to the United States
Placing them with the Guggenheim family on Long Island, the baroness
Then somehow rejoined her husband in Africa with the Free French
Serving in various capacities including ambulance driver and ending

SWING, HARD BOP, BOP & BEBOP

The war as a decorated lieutenant, her husband's extended family
As well as her own mother were nearly all killed in the Holocaust
The baroness's adoption of New York's predominantly black jazz
Family in the war's aftermath thus seems less the act of a suspect dabbler
Than of a survivor bent on resurrection and rebirth, she could no longer
Live in any ivory tower after what she saw in the war -
Privilege offered No protection -
The fate of her own mother-in-law proved that, she had
Experienced the very depths of prejudice herself firsthand

The baroness credited her brother, a jazz fan with introducing her to jazz.
She said that the moment she heard Monk's "Straight, No Chaser"
Was the moment her interest in jazz music escalated into something more
"I belonged where that music was, this was something I was supposed
To be involved in in some way," the baroness first materialized in
New York jazz clubs in the early 1950s like some film noir siren, right
Down to the raven hair and Long cigarette holder, she seduced the music's
Greatest figures with her friendship, the revolutionists of the bebop era
Charlie Parker, Dizzy Gillespie, Miles Davis, Thelonious Monk and many others
Caused her illustrious family to refuse to discuss her

It is well known in jazz circles that the great project of the baroness's
Life was the torturously unstable Monk, whom she served as a surrogate
Wife right alongside Monk's equally devoted actual wife, Nellie. The
Baroness paid Monk's bills, dragged him to an endless array of doctors
Put him and his family up in her own home and, when necessary, helped
Nellie institutionalize him, in 1958 Monk and the baroness were stopped
By the police in Delaware when a small amount of marijuana was discovered
She took the rap for her friend and even served a few nights in jail

Baroness Pannonica de Koenigswarter died on November 30, 1988, but
Lives through the numerous compositions in her honor Gigi Gryce's
Nica's Tempo, Sonny Clark's *Nica*, Horace Silver's *Nica's Dream*,
Kenny Dorham's *To Nica*, Kenny Drew's *Blues for Nica*, Freddie Redd's
Nica Steps Out, Barry Harris's *Inca*, Tommy Flanagan's *Thelonica*,
And Thelonious Monk's *Pannonica*, were all named after her.

Thelonious Sphere Monk

I was floored when Charlie Rico
Brought him to my room (in my mother's house)
I played a recording he made with
The 'Trane
He pranced to the beat
And recreated his riff
Only one of five jazzmen
To grace the cover of Time
Magazine pioneer in bebop
We spoke then they left.

I was 21, just out of the army
Making a hustle until I found
Work

Monk was exceptional in many things
Math, physics and Ping-Pong and
It's cool that he referred to himself as
The-onlyest Monk

Monk rose from Minton's Playhouse
'Round Midnight
Using silence and hesitation
In a style never heard before
Made them go Straight No Chaser
I remembered our conversation
Then
In Walked Bud.

SWING, HARD BOP, BOP & BEBOP

Max Roach

Maxwell Lemuel Roach, was born on January 10, 1924, in New Land
North Carolina, he was raised in Brooklyn and played in gospel groups
As a child, though he started on the piano, Roach found his instrument
When he began playing the drums at age 10, Roach is generally
Considered among the most important drummers in history, he was a
Pioneer of bebop and worked with many famous jazz musicians, including
Coleman Hawkins, Dizzy Gillespie, Charlie Parker, Miles Davis
Duke Ellington, Thelonious Monk, Abbey Lincoln, Dinah Washington
Charles Mingus, Billy Eckstine, Stan Getz, Sonny Rollins, Eric Dolphy
And Booker Little, he was inducted into the Down Beat Hall of Fame in
1980 and the *Modern Drummer* Hall of Fame in 1992

Roach also led his own groups, notably a pioneering quintet co-led with
Trumpeter Clifford Brown, Max Roach made numerous musical statements
Relating to the Civil Rights Movement, in 1960 he composed and recorded
The album *We Insist!* subtitled *Max Roach's Freedom Now Suite*, with vocals
By his then-wife Abbey Lincoln and lyrics by Oscar Brown Jr., after being
Invited to contribute to commemorations of the hundredth anniversary of
Abraham Lincoln's Emancipation Proclamation, in 1962, he recorded the album
Money Jungle, a collaboration with Mingus and Duke Ellington, this is
Generally regarded as one of the very finest trio albums ever made

In the early 1980s, Roach began presenting entire concerts solo, proving that
This multi-percussion instrument could fulfill the demands of solo performance
And be entirely satisfying to an audience, he created memorable compositions
In these solo concerts; a solo record was released by Baystate, a Japanese label

Roach wrote music for theater, such as plays written by Sam Shepard
Presented at La Mama E.T.C. in New York City, his other collaborators
Included hip-hop artists Fab Five Freddy, writer Toni Morrison, Roach
Provided musical accompaniment at her spoken word concerts
Japanese taiko drummers and avant-garde instrumentalists Cecil Taylor
And Anthony Braxton

HORACE MUNGIN

Roach gave his last concert in 2000 and made his final recording in 2002
He suffered from a neurological disorder for an extended period before
His death in New York City on August 16, 2007, at the age of 83.

SWING, HARD BOP, BOP & BEBOP

Ahmad Jamal

One of the most individualistic pianists, composers, and arrangers
Of his generation, Ahmad Jamal's disciplined technique and minimalist
Style had a huge impact on trumpeter Miles Davis, and Jamal is often
Cited as contributing to the development of cool jazz throughout the 1950s

Ahmad Jamal was born Frederick Russell Jones, July 2, 1930, Pittsburgh
Pennsylvania, Jamal began formal piano training at the age of seven
His Pittsburgh roots have remained an important part of his identity
It was there that he was absorbed in the influence of jazz artists such
As Earl Hines, Billy Strayhorn, Mary Lou Williams, and Erroll Garner

Jamal discovered Islam in his early 20s, while touring in Detroit
Where there was a sizable Muslim community in the 1940's and 1950's
He became interested in Islam and Islamic culture, he converted to
Islam and changed his name to Ahmad Jamal in 1950, He made his
First records in 1951 for the *Okeh* label with The Three Strings
Which would later also be called the Ahmad Jamal Trio, the Three
Strings arranged an extended engagement at Chicago's Blue Note
But leapt to fame after performing at the Embers in New York City
John Hammond saw the band play and signed them to *Okeh* Records
Hammond, a record producer, helped Jamal's trio attract critical acclaim

Jamal's most famous recording and undoubtedly the one that brought him
Vast popularity in the late 1950s and into the 1960s jazz age, was recorded
At the Pershing Hotel in Chicago in 1958, Jamal played the set with bassist
Israel Crosby and drummer Vernel Fournier, the set list expressed a diverse
Collection of tunes, including *The Surrey with the Fringe On Top* from the
Musical *Oklahoma!* and Jamal's arrangement of the jazz standard *Poinciana*

After the recording of the best-selling album *But Not For Me*, Jamal's music
Grew in popularity throughout the 1950s, in 1959, he took a tour of North
Africa to explore investment options in Africa, upon his return to the U.S.
After a tour of North Africa, the financial success of *Live at the Pershing
But Not For Me* allowed Jamal to open a restaurant and club called The

HORACE MUNGIN

Alhambra in Chicago, in 1962, The Three Strings disbanded and Jamal Moved to New York City, where, at the age of 32, he took a three-year Hiatus from his musical career

In 1964, Jamal resumed touring and recording, in 1986, Jamal sued critic Leonard Feather for using his former name in a publication, now in his Eighties, Ahmad Jamal has continued to make numerous tours and recordings His most recently released album is *Saturday Morning* (2013).

Nina Simone

I had no idea the complexity
Of her intricate existence
Once driving with a musician
Who worked with her
She came up next on the CD
I played during our drive
On hearing her voice my companion
Made a foul comment in Nina's name

I knew her only as a weaver of spells
And a civil rights Activist

Nothing about her demons
Had ever reached my ears
Nothing of her conflict with
Her colleagues
Nothing about her abusive
Husband or
How she abused her daughter

Oh, I did know that racism held
Her back from pursuing European
Classical music – she was too dark
Her lips too full, her nose too large
Her hair too stringy, her purse too
Empty

Now I see how deep the resentment
Cut into her soul and made her life
A battleground fermenting the flame
And the fury I hear in her music.

One Woman
(For Nina Simone)

It was 1957 I heard you sing
About loving Porgy your voice
Claiming the love and anguish
Of our struggling tribe
I fell instantly in love with
Your voice, your music and you.

I said hello to you on Lenox Avenue
In 1968 the year the world ended
I cherished your concerts from
Front row seats at the Apollo Theater

I wish I knew how it feels to be free
I wish I could break all the chains holding me

I closed my eyes and wandered
Through your defiant rejection
Of humiliation and injustice
Your passionate rendition of
The songs of our traditions
You stretched creative arrangements
To take a great music to higher heights
And I heard in your voice – my voice

The Sun's gonna shine in
My back backdoor
Someday.

SWING, HARD BOP, BOP & BEBOP

Eddie Harris

Eddie Harris was born October 20, 1934, in Chicago
Eddie Harris studied music under Walter Dyett
At DuSable High School, he was proficient on piano
Vibraphone, and tenor saxophone, in 1969 he performed
With pianist and vocalist Les McCann at the Montreux
Jazz Festival, although the musicians had been unable to
Rehearse, their session was so impressive that a recording
Of it was released by Atlantic as *Swiss Movement*

Eddie had a musical harmonic figure that stayed
With him his whole career –
You hear it in Listen Here and Cold Duck Time
It was a call and answer sound he played with variations

– a cool cat,
Eddie liked to talk on his recordings
He also started singing comic R&B/blues songs
Such as *That is Why You're Overweight* and *Eddie Who?*
In 1975, however, he alienated much of his audience with
His album *The Reason Why I'm Talking Shit*
Which consisted mainly of comedy

Or, take the irony of his Bad Luck tail, or
His telling of the time he was asked
Who was appearing at the club that night
He told the inquirer – Eddie Harris
And his voice delights as he repeats her
Retort – Eddie who? I ain't never heard of him
Can he play?
He picked up his horn and played the
First stanza of *Listen Here*.

Sarah Vaughn

Sarah Lois Vaughan born March 27, 1924
In Newark, New Jersey

Sassy, sultry Sarah, the Divine One
Operatic range and soothing tones
Served as the silky ageless sound of
Modern jazz and one of the most
Wondrous voices of the 20th century

Sarah began piano lessons at the age of
Seven, sang in the church choir and
Occasionally played piano for rehearsals
And church services, her voice was a gift
She honed it to fit the sound of the golden
Age of 1950's cool jazz, Vaughan was
A four-time Grammy Award winner
Including a Lifetime Achievement Award

Vaughan began her solo career in 1945 by
Freelancing in clubs on New York's 52nd Street
Such as the Three Deuces, the Famous Door
The Downbeat and the Onyx Club, Vaughan hung
Around the Braddock Grill, next to the Apollo
Theater in Harlem

Parallels have been drawn between Vaughan's voice
And that of opera singers but even more, Sarah molded
The classics of Cole Porter, Johnny Mercer
Irving Berlin and other great songwriters into
Her own creations with sentimental clarity
And lyrical diction.

SWING, HARD BOP, BOP & BEBOP

Sun Ra

In tomorrow's world, men will not need artificial instruments such as jets and space ships. In the world of tomorrow, the new man will 'think' the place he wants to go, then his mind will take him there. -- Sun Ra, 1956

Sun Ra was raised by his aunt and grandmother, 'Sonny' as he
Was nicknamed, received a piano for his seventh birthday and
With little musical training, he taught himself to read music

Sun Ra claimed that he was sent to earth from outer space
To save humanity and bring harmony to the world, besides
Being from Saturn, Ra came from the tradition of vaudeville
Swing, and Chicago show clubs, he was also deeply spiritual
And his live shows encompassed all of these elements, they
Were several hour ritualistic ceremonies featuring a hot
Arkestra of a dozen players, poetry, light shows, dancers
Marches through the audience, and shrieking sax solos
Sometimes the band members would take the stage to
The chant of "Heigh-ho, heigh ho, it's off to work we go"

It is rumored that Sun Ra, was born Herman Blount in Birmingham
Alabama, He formed his own band in high School, Sonny went to
Alabama A&M on a scholarship where he led the student band
He would transcribe the popular swing band tunes from the radio
And soon have his band playing them, around this time he claimed
That he had been transported into a spaceship by aliens, who
Informed him of his higher calling, during World War II, Sonny
Blount was jailed for being a conscientious objector, he was so
Absorbed in music and his inquiries in ancient black cultures and
So contrary to violence was he that combat was unimaginable to him

He left Birmingham for good after the war and moved to Chicago
Where he was hired as the practice pianist at the popular and glamorous
Club DeLisa, which featured showgirls, comedians, singers, and floor shows
At the DeLisa he got to work with his hero, Fletcher Henderson, one of

HORACE MUNGIN

The creators of the swing sound, Sun Ra worked as a pianist/arranger
With Fletcher Henderson in 1946 and 1947, he also performed with swing
Musicians Coleman Hawkins and Stuff Smith in 1948, but really got
Started around 1953 leading a big band he called the Arkestra in Chicago
Ra started off playing advanced bop, but early on he was open to the
Influences of other cultures, his live shows were like religious ceremonies
Ra was incorporating odd instruments into the Arkestra's sound, like zithers
Timbales, chimes, claves, all kinds of bells and gongs, and things with names
Like "solar drum," "space lute," and "boom bam." He also had the Arkestra
Wearing space costumes, like helmets with flashing lights and propellers
Some of the costumes were hand-me-downs from a Chicago opera company
Some were made by culinary guru Vertamae Smart-Grosvenor and the women who
Stage danced in his shows, Ra built the ensemble up to full strength with
New York musicians and began to attract attention, he was part of the
New "free jazz" revolution taking place in Greenwich Village in the '60s along
With John Coltrane and others, the mid-'60s, Sun Ra and the Arkestra weren't just
Visiting outer space; it was their permanent habitat, the music had become
A ghostly blend of dissonant, unusual sounds and effects, Sun Ra had
Transformed his eccentric big band of hard bop soloists into an experimental
Open-improvisation ensemble, Ra was becoming the philosopher-king of
Afro-psychedelia, Ra's music of this period was typified by counter melodies
Off-key horn barrages, polyrhythms, titanic organ and synthesizer solos and
Harsh note clusters

Albums appearing on popular labels exposed Sun Ra's work to post-punk/indie
Audiences, Ra became a fixture of Philadelphia radio stations and regularly
Gave lectures, he appeared on Hal Willner's tribute album *Stay Awake* in 1988
Sun Ra died in 1993 leaving the following verse for us all.

In some far-off place
Many light years in space
I'll build a world of abstract dreams
And wait for you

SWING, HARD BOP, BOP & BEBOP

Dexter Gordon

Dexter Gordon was nominated for an Academy Award for Best Actor in
His very first acting role for his performance in the 1986 film *Round Midnight*
He won a Grammy for Best Jazz Instrumental Performance, Soloist for the
Soundtrack album (Blue Note Records, 1986) *The Other Side of Round Midnight*
Dexter acted with the same intensity he applied to his horn and it was noticed

Dexter's father, Dr. Frank Gordon, was one of the first African American
Doctors in Los Angeles, he arrived in 1918 after graduating from Howard
Medical School in Washington, D.C., Dexter's maternal grandfather, Captain
Edward Baker, received the Medal of Honor in the Spanish–American War
Dexter Keith Gordon was born on February 27, 1923 in Los Angeles, California

Gordon played clarinet from the age of 13, before switching to saxophone
Initially alto, then tenor at 15, while still at school, he played in bands with
Such contemporaries as Chico Hamilton and Buddy Collette, between
December 1940 and 1943, Gordon was a member of Lionel Hampton's band
Playing in a saxophone section alongside Illinois Jacquet and Marshal Royal
During 1944 he was featured in the Fletcher Henderson band, followed by
The Louis Armstrong band, before going to New York City to join Billy
Eckstine's orchestra with his large, spacious sound, Dexter was known as
The Sophisticated Giant because of his 6 feet 6 inches tall lean body
– some called him Long-tail Dexter

By late 1945 he was recording under his own name for the Savoy label in 1947
Dexter was leading sessions for Ross Russell's Dial label after his return to Los
Angeles he became known for his saxophone duels with fellow tenor man Wardell
Gray, which were a popular concert attraction documented in recordings made
Between 1947 and 1952, then gained literary fame from its mention in Jack Kerouac's
Book *On The Road*, which also has images of wild tenor men jamming in Los
Angeles

Gordon recorded with Dizzy Gillespie and as a leader for Savoy before returning
To Los Angeles in the summer of 1946, he was a major part of the Central Avenue
Scene, trading off with Wardell Gray and Teddy Edwards in many legendary tenor
Battles, the 1950s, Gordon's recorded output and live appearances declined as heroin

HORACE MUNGIN

Addiction and legal troubles took their toll, Gordon signed to Blue Note Records
In 1961, he initially commuted from Los Angeles to New York to record, but took
Up residence when he regained the cabaret card that allowed him to perform where
Alcohol was served; The Jazz Gallery hosted his first New York performance in
Twelve years, Dexter spent the next twelve years living mainly in Paris and
Copenhagen, and played regularly with fellow expatriates and visiting musicians

Gordon visited the US occasionally for further recording dates *Gettin' Around*
Was recorded for Blue Note during a visit in May 1965, as was the album *Clubhouse*
Which remained unreleased until 1979, Gordon found Europe in the 1960s a much
Easier place to live, saying that he experienced less racism and greater respect for
Jazz musicians, he also stated that on his visits to the US in the late 1960s and early
1970's, he found the political and social strife disturbing

Gordon finally returned to the United States for good in 1976, he appeared with
Woody Shaw, Ronnie Mathews, Stafford James, and Louis Hayes, for a gig at the
Village Vanguard in New York that was dubbed his "homecoming," the session was
Recorded and released by Columbia Records under that title, in 1978 and 1980
Gordon was the Down Beat Musician of the Year and in 1980 he was inducted
Into the Jazz Hall of Fame, the US Government honored him with a Congressional
Commendation, a Dexter Gordon Day in Washington DC, and a National
Endowment for the Arts award for Lifetime Achievement, in 1986, he was named
A member and officer of the French Order of Arts and Letters by the Ministry of
Culture in France, During the 1980's, Gordon was weakened by emphysema, he
Remained a popular attraction at concerts and festivals, although his live appearances
And recording dates would soon become infrequent, Gordon died of kidney failure
And cancer of the larynx in Philadelphia, on April 25, 1990, at the age of 67.

SWING, HARD BOP, BOP & BEBOP

Sonny Rollins

Walter Theodore Rollins was born in New York City
In September 7, 1930 to immigrant parents from the
United States Virgin Island, he grew up in central
Harlem and Sugar Hill, graduated from Benjamin Franklin
High School in East Harlem, Rollins started as a pianist
He switched to alto, then tenor sax in 1946, he played
In a band during his high school years with future
Jazz legends Jackie McLean and Art Taylor

After graduating from high school in 1947
Rollins began performing professionally
He made his first recordings in early 1949
As a sideman with the bebop singer Babs Gonzales
He began to make a name for himself, recording
With J. J. Johnson and appearing under the leadership
Of pianist Bud Powell, alongside trumpeter Fats Navarro
And drummer Roy Haynes, on a seminal "hard bop" session

In early 1950, Rollins was arrested for armed robbery
And spent ten months in Rikers Island jail before being
Released on parole; in 1952, he was re-arrested for violating
The terms of his parole by using heroin, between 1951 and 1953
He recorded with Miles Davis, the Modern Jazz Quartet
Charlie Parker, and Thelonious Monk, He achieved a
Breakthrough in 1954 when he recorded his famous
Compositions with a quintet led by Davis that also
Featured pianist Horace Silver

In 1956 Rollins made his biggest move, joining the famous ensemble
Of Max Roach and Clifford Brown, then formed his own legendary
Piano-less trio with bassist Wilbur Ware and drummer Elvin Jones in 1957
Recording sessions at the Village Vanguard brought awards from
Down Beat and Playboy magazines, these recordings were done mainly
For the Prestige and Riverside labels, but also for Verve, Blue Note

HORACE MUNGIN

Columbia, and Contemporary Records, all coinciding with the steadily
Rising star of Rollins

Between 1959 and 1961 he sought a less superficial, more spiritual
Path to the rat race society of the times, Rollins had become frustrated
With what he perceived as his own musical limitations and took a musical
Sabbatical visiting Japan and India and studying yoga and Zen
He left the music business until 1962, on his return, he lived on the
Lower East Side of Manhattan, he ventured to the pedestrian walkway of
The Williamsburg Bridge to practice, in the summer of 1961, the journalist
Ralph Berton happened to pass by the saxophonist on the bridge one day
And he published an article in *Metronome* magazine about the occurrence

Rollins named his 1962 "comeback" album *The Bridge,* the disc was recorded
With a quartet featuring guitarist Jim Hall, Ben Riley on drums, and bassist
Bob Crenshaw, this became one of Rollins's best-selling records, in 2015
It was inducted into the Grammy Hall of Fame, Rollins' career rolled on
Strong into the twentieth first century performing the world over
On September 11, 2001, the 71-year-old Rollins, who lived several blocks
Away, heard the World Trade Center collapse, and was forced to
Evacuate his apartment, with only his saxophone in hand, Rollins was
Presented with a Grammy Award for lifetime achievement in 2004
That year also saw the death of his wife, Lucille

In 2013, Rollins moved to Woodstock, New York that spring he made
A guest television appearance on *The Simpsons* and received an honorary
Doctor of Music degree from the Juilliard School in New York City
Rollins has not performed since 2012, due to recurring respiratory issues
In 2014 he was the subject of a Dutch television documentary entitled
Sonny Rollins-Morgen Speel ik Beter and in October 2015, he received
The Jazz Foundation of America's lifetime achievement award in the spring
Of 2017, Rollins donated his personal archive to the Schomburg Center for
Research in Black Culture, a branch of the New York Public Library
Sonny Rollins is one of only two survivors of the 57 musicians in that famous
1958 picture "A Great Day in Harlem," the other is tenor saxophonist Benny Golson.

Paul Desmond

Best known for his work with the Dave Brubeck Quartet and
For composing that group's biggest hit, *Take Five,* Paul Desmond
Was born Paul Emil Breitenfeld, November 25, 1924, in San Francisco
California. In addition to his work with Brubeck, he led several groups
And collaborated with Gerry Mulligan and Chet Baker

Desmond began to study clarinet at the age of twelve, which he
Continued while at San Francisco Polytechnic High School
It was not until he became a freshman at San Francisco State College
That he picked up the alto saxophone, in his first year Desmond was
Drafted into the United States Army and joined the Army band while
Stationed in San Francisco, Desmond had first met Dave Brubeck in
1944 while still in the military, Brubeck was trying out for the 253rd
Army band which Desmond already belonged to

His last concert was with Brubeck in February 1977, in New York City
His fans did not know that he was dying, Desmond would sometimes
Need a vitamin B12 shot just to go on playing during his later career
After years of chain smoking and poor health, Desmond succumbed
To lung cancer in 1977 following one last tour with Brubeck.

HORACE MUNGIN

Hank Mobley

Mobley was born July 30, 1930 in Eastman, Georgia, but was raised in
Elizabeth, New Jersey, near Newark, when he was 16, an illness kept him
In the house for several months, his grandmother bought him a saxophone
To help him occupy his time, he wanted to go to music school, but because
He didn't live in Newark he was unable register there, so he taught himself
By studying through books at home, at 19, he started to play with local
Bands and later worked for the first time with Dizzy Gillespie and Max Roach
He took part in one of the earliest hard bop sessions, alongside Art Blakey
Horace Silver, Doug Watkins and trumpeter Kenny Dorham, making him one
Of the youngest beboppers, with the luck of having arrived on the scene on time

These sessions were released as *Horace Silver and the Jazz Messengers,*
They contrasted with the classical inclinations of cool jazz, with Mobley's
Rich bluesy lyricism alongside the funky approach of Silver, when the
Jazz Messengers split in 1956, Mobley continued on with pianist Silver
For a short time, although he did work again with Blakey some years later
When the drummer appeared on Mobley's albums in the early 1960s

During the 1960s, he worked chiefly as a leader, recording over 20 albums
For Blue Note Records between 1955 and 1970, these were generally considered
To be his finest recordings, he performed with many of the other important hard
Bop players, such as Grant Green, Freddie Hubbard, Sonny Clark, Wynton Kelly
And Philly Joe Jones, and formed a particularly productive partnership with
Trumpeter Lee Morgan, Mobley is widely recognized as one of the great composers
Of originals in the hard bop era, with interesting chord changes and room for
Soloists to stretch out

Mobley spent a brief time in 1961 with Miles Davis, during the trumpeter's search
For a replacement for John Coltrane, he is heard on the album *Someday My Prince
Will Come,* Mobley was forced to retire in the mid-1970's due to lung problems
He worked two engagements at the Angry Squire in New York City November 22
And 23, 1985, and January 11, 1986, in a quartet with Duke Jordan a few months
Before his death from pneumonia in 1986.

SWING, HARD BOP, BOP & BEBOP

Lee Morgan

Edward Lee Morgan was born in Philadelphia, Pennsylvania in July 10, 1938, He came to prominence as a hard bop musician at the Early age of 18, he recorded with John Coltrane in 1957 and with Art Blakey before he went on his own solo career, He recorded as A leader in the 60's, his recording "Sidewinder" became a surprise Crossover hit on the pop and R&B charts in 1964, his work for Blue Note with the likes of Hank Mobley and Wayne Shorter made Him a cornerstone of the label

Lee Morgan's career was cut short at the age 33, when his Common-law wife shot him to death following a skirmish At the popular Slug's Saloon on Manhattan's the Lower East Side.

Wes Montgomery
(For Mark Melcher)

John Leslie "Wes" Montgomery was born March 6, 1923
He was an American jazz guitarist, widely considered one
Of the major jazz guitarists, emerging after such seminal
Figures as Django Reinhardt and Charlie Christian, Wes
Often worked with his brothers Buddy (piano and vibes)
And Monk (bass guitar), and with organist Jimmy Smith

Wes' recordings up to 1965 were generally oriented towards
Hard bop, while after 1965 he began recording more pop-oriented
Instrumental albums that featured less improvisation still but found
Mainstream success, Wes was born in Indianapolis, Indiana
His nickname "Wes" was a childhood abbreviation of his
Middle name, Leslie, although he was not skilled at reading
Music, he could learn complex melodies and riffs by ear
Wes started learning the six-string guitar at the relatively late
Age of 20 by listening to and learning the recordings of his idol
Guitarist Charlie Christian

SWING, HARD BOP, BOP & BEBOP

Wes toured with Lionel Hampton early in his career
But the combined stress of touring and being away from
Family took him back home to Indianapolis, to support
His family of eight, Wes worked in a factory from 7:00 am
To 3:00 pm, then performed in local clubs from 9:00 pm to 2:00 am
Cannonball Adderley heard Montgomery in an Indianapolis club
And was so impressed, the next morning, he called record producer
Orrin Keepnews, who signed Montgomery to a recording contract
With Riverside Records, Adderley later recorded with Wes on his
Pollwinners album. Wes recorded with his brothers as the
Montgomery Brothers and with various other group members

On the morning of June 15, 1968, Wes awoke not feeling very well
He soon collapsed, dying of a heart attack within minutes, 45 years
Old at the time of his death, Montgomery had just returned from a
Tour with his quintet and was at the height of his fame, having attained
A degree of popular acceptance that few jazz artists in that era achieved
Wes Montgomery's home town of Indianapolis named a park in his honor.

Rahsaan Roland Kirk

Kirk was born Ronald Theodore, but he had dreams
About name changes, in one dream he was instructed
To reconfigure Ronald to Roland, another dream told
Him to add Rahsaan, Kirk was born August 7, 1935 in
Columbus, Ohio, he was born with sight, but became
Blind at the age of two due to bad medical care, Kirk began
Playing tenor sax professionally in R&B bands at the age of 15

Kirk collected and played a number of musical instruments
Mainly various saxophones, clarinets and flutes, his main
Instruments were tenor saxophone supplemented by other saxes
Like two obscure saxophones: the stritch, a straight alto sax
Missing the instrument's characteristic upturned bell and a
Manzello, a modified saxello soprano sax, with a larger upturned
Bell, a number of his instruments were exotic or homemade

SWING, HARD BOP, BOP & BEBOP

He typically appeared on stage with all three horns hanging
Around his neck and at times he would play a number of
These horns at once, harmonizing with himself, or sustaining
A note for lengthy durations by using a circular breathing technique
He should have received credit in
The Guinness Book of World Records
For such feats – but his playing was generally rooted in soul jazz
Or hard bop, but Kirk's knowledge of jazz history allowed him to
Draw from many elements of the music's past, from ragtime to
Swing and free jazz, the live Album *Bright Moments* (1973)
Is an example of one of his shows

Kirk was politically outspoken, during his concerts, between songs
He often talked about topical issues, including African-American
History and the Civil Rights Movement, his monologues were often
Laced with satire and absurdist humor, when comedian Jay Leno toured
With Kirk as his opening act, Kirk would introduce him by saying
"I want to introduce a young brother who knows the black experience
And knows all about the white devils ... Please welcome Jay Leno"

HORACE MUNGIN

Les McCann

Leslie Coleman McCann, was born September 23, 1935
In Lexington, Kentucky, he is an American jazz pianist
And vocalist, musical success for McCann came early
When he won a Navy talent contest for singing; this led
To an appearance on the Ed Sullivan Show, McCann's
Main career began in the early 1960's when he recorded
As a pianist with his trio for Pacific Jazz Records

In 1969, Atlantic Records released *Swiss Movement*
A recording of McCann with his regular collaborator
Saxophonist Eddie Harris, the album contained the
Song "Compared to What", and both the album and
The single were huge *Billboard* pop chart successes
"Compared to What" featured political criticism of
The unpopular Vietnam War

After the success of *Swiss Movement*, McCann, primarily
A piano player, began to emphasize his rough-hewn
Vocals more, he became an innovator in the soul-jazz style
Merging jazz with funk, soul and world rhythms, he was
Among the first jazz musicians to include electric piano
Clavinet, and synthesizer in his music

In 1971, he and Harris were part of a group of soul, R&B
And rock performers, including Wilson Pickett, the Staple Singers
Santana and Ike & Tina Turner – who flew to Accra, Ghana
For a historic 14-hour concert before more than 100,000
Ghanaians, the March 6 concert was recorded for the
Documentary film *Soul To Soul*, in 2004 the movie was
Released on DVD with an accompanying soundtrack album

SWING, HARD BOP, BOP & BEBOP

Les McCann discovered Roberta Flack and arranged an
Audition which resulted in a recording contract for her
With Atlantic Records, a mild stroke in the mid-1990's
Sidelined McCann for a while but in 2002 he released
A new album, *Pump it Up*, McCann has also exhibited
As a painter and photographer.

HORACE MUNGIN

Herbie Hancock

Herbert Jeffrey "Herbie" Hancock was born in Chicago
Illinois April 12, 1940, he turned out to be one of the
Primary architects of the post-bop sound, Hancock's music is
Often melodic and accessible; he has had many songs
cross-over and achieve success among pop audiences
His parents named him after the singer and actor Herb Jeffries
An African-American actor of film and television and popular
Music and jazz singer-songwriter, known for his baritone voice
He was Hollywood's first black singing cowboy

Like many jazz pianists, Hancock started with a classical music
Education, he studied from age seven, and his talent was recognized
Early, considered a child prodigy he played the first movement of
Mozart's Piano Concerto No. 26 in D Major, at a young people's
Concert on February 5, 1952, with the Chicago Symphony Orchestra
Led by CSO assistant conductor George Schick, at the age of 11
Through his teens, Hancock never had a jazz teacher, but developed
His ear and sense of harmony by listening to jazz recordings

After studies at Grinnell College, Hancock was invited by Donald Byrd
In 1961 to join his group in New York City, and before long, Blue Note
Offered him a solo contract his debut album, Takin' Off, took off after
Mongo Santamaria covered one of the album's songs, "Watermelon Man"
In May 1963, Miles Davis asked him to join his band in time for the
Seven Steps to Heaven sessions, and he remained with him for five
Years, greatly influencing Miles' evolving direction

Hancock loosening up his own style, upon Davis' suggestion, converting
To the Rhodes electric piano during that time, Hancock's solo career
Blossomed on Blue Note, as he poured forth increasingly sophisticated
Compositions like "Maiden Voyage," "Cantaloupe Island,"
"Goodbye to Childhood," and the exquisite "Speak Like a Child".
He provided a groundbreaking score to Michelangelo Antonioni's film
Blow Up, which gradually led to additional movie assignments

SWING, HARD BOP, BOP & BEBOP

In 1969 Hancock formed a sextet that evolved into one of the most exciting
Forward-looking jazz-rock groups of the era, by 1970, all of the musicians
Used both English and African names, Herbie's was Mwandishi, Sadly
Hancock had to break up the band in 1973 when it ran out of money
And having studied Buddhism, he concluded that his ultimate goal should
Be to make his audiences happy

After the sometimes "airy" and decidedly experimental "*Mwandishi*" albums
Hancock was eager to perform more "earthy" and "funky" music, the
Mwandishi albums – though later seen as respected early fusion recordings
had seen mixed reviews and poor sales, so it is probable that Hancock was
Motivated by financial concerns as well as artistic restlessness, Hancock was
Also bothered by the fact that many people did not understand avant-garde
Music, he explained that he loved funk music, especially Sly Stone's music
So, he wanted to try to make funk himself

He gathered a new band, which he called The Headhunters, keeping only
Maupin from the sextet and adding bassist Paul Jackson, percussionist Bill
Summers, and drummer Harvey Mason, the album *Head Hunters*, released
In 1973, was a major hit and crossed over to pop audiences, though it
Prompted criticism from some jazz fans.

Hancock also released a solo acoustic piano album, *The Piano* (1979), which
Was released only in Japan. It was later released in the US in 2004, other Japan
only albums include *Dedication* (1974), *V.S.O.P.'s Tempest in the Colosseum*
(1977), and *Direct Step* (1978). *VSOP: Live Under the Sky* was a VSOP album
Remastered for the US in 2004 and included a second concert from the tour in
July 1979, since 1972, Hancock has practiced Nichiren Buddhism as a member
Of the Buddhist association Soka Gakkai International, as part of Hancock's
Spiritual practice, he recites the Buddhist chant *Nam Myoho Renge Kyo* each day
In 2013, Hancock's dialogue with musician Wayne Shorter and Soka Gakkai
International president Daisaku Ikeda on jazz, Buddhism and life was
Published in Japanese

Hancock is the 2014 Charles Eliot Norton Professor of Poetry at Harvard University
Holders of the chair deliver a series of six lectures on poetry, "The Norton Lectures"
Poetry being interpreted in the broadest sense, including all poetic expression in
Language, music, or fine arts, previous Norton lecturers include musicians
Leonard Bernstein, Igor Stravinsky and John Cage
Hancock's theme is The Ethics of Jazz.

HORACE MUNGIN

Red Garland

William McKinley "Red" Garland, Jr. born May 13, 1923 in Dallas, Texas
Garland helped popularize the block chord style of piano playing, he began
His musical studies on the clarinet and alto saxophone but, in 1941
Switched to the piano, five years later Garland joined a well-known
Trumpet player in the southwest - Hot Lips Page, playing with him until
A tour ended in New York in March 1946, Garland decided to stay in
New York City to find work, Art Blakey came across Garland playing at
A small club, only to return the next night with Blakey's boss, Billy Eckstine

Garland performed with Billy Eckstine, Roy Eldridge, Coleman Hawkins
Charlie Parker, and Lester Young, he found steady work in the cities of Boston
New York City, and Philadelphia, in the late 1940's, he toured with Eddie Vinson
At the same time that John Coltrane was in Vinson's band, his creativity and
Playing ability continued to improve, though he was still somewhat obscure
By the time he became a pianist for Miles Davis, he had been influenced by
Ahmad Jamal and Charlie Parker's pianist Walter Bishop

Garland also had a short-lived career as a welterweight boxer in the 1940's
He fought more than 35 fights, one being an exhibition bout with
Sugar Ray Robinson, Garland became famous in 1954 when he joined
The Miles Davis Quintet, featuring John Coltrane, Philly Joe Jones
And Paul Chambers, Davis was a fan of boxing and was impressed that
Garland had boxed earlier in his life, together, the group recorded their
Famous Prestige albums, *Miles: The New Miles Davis Quintet* (1954)
Workin'!, *Steamin'*, *Cookin'*, and *Relaxin'*, Garland's style is prominent in
These seminal recordings, evident in his distinctive chord voicings
His sophisticated accompaniment, his musical references to Ahmad Jamal's style

SWING, HARD BOP, BOP & BEBOP

In 1958, Garland formed his own trio. Among the musicians the trio recorded
With are Pepper Adams, Nat Adderley, Ray Barretto, Kenny Burrell
Eddie "Lockjaw" Davis, Jimmy Heath, Harold Land, Philly Joe Jones, Blue
Mitchell, Ira Sullivan, and Leroy Vinnegar, the trio also recorded as a quintet
With John Coltrane and Donald Byrd, Altogether, Garland led 19 recording
Sessions while at Prestige Records and 25 sessions for Fantasy Records
He stopped playing professionally for a number of years in the 1960's when
The popularity of rock music coincided with a substantial drop in the popularity
Of jazz, He continued recording until his death from a heart attack on April
23, 1984 at the age of 60.

HORACE MUNGIN

Abbey Lincoln

Anna Marie Wooldridge Born in Chicago but raised in Cass County, Michigan
She went through several name changes including Anna Marie, Gaby Lee, and
Gaby Woolridge before settling on Abbey Lincoln. She was born August 6, 1930
As with her hero Billie Holiday, Abbey Lincoln always meant the lyrics she sang
A dramatic performer whose interpretations were full of truth and insight, she wrote
And performed her own compositions, she was a civil rights advocate and activist
From the 1960's on, Lincoln made a career not only out of delivering deeply felt
Presentations of standards but writing and singing her own material as well

Her debut album, *Abbey Lincoln's Affair – A Story of a Girl in Love*, was followed
By a series of albums for Riverside Records, in 1960 she sang on Max Roach's
Landmark civil rights-themed recording, *We Insist!* Lincoln's lyrics were often
Connected to the civil rights movement in America

During the 1980s, Lincoln's creative output was smaller; she fulfilled a 10-album
Contract with Verve Records, after a tour of Africa in the mid-1970's, she adopted
The name Aminata Moseka, the album that is highly regarded and represents the
Crowning achievement in Lincoln's career is *Devil's Got Your Tongue* (1992)
Featured Rodney Kendrick, Grady Tate, J. J. Johnson, Stanley Turrentine
Babatunde Olatunji and The Staple Singers, among others

Her lyrics often reflected the ideals of the civil rights movement and helped
In generating passion for the cause in the minds of her listeners, in addition
To her musical career, she ventured into acting as well and appeared in movies
Such as *The Girl Can't Help It* and *Gentleman Prefer Blondes*, she explored
More philosophical themes during the later years of her songwriting career
And remained professionally active until well into her seventies

She co-starred with Ivan Dixon in *Nothing But a Man* (1964)
Lincoln was married from 1962 to 1970 to drummer Max Roach
Lincoln died on August 14, 2010 in Manhattan, eight days after
Her 80th birthday.

SWING, HARD BOP, BOP & BEBOP

Stan Getz

Stan Getz was known as "The Sound" because of his warm, lyrical tone
His prime influence was the fine mellow timbre of his idol, Lester Young
Getz was born Stanley Gayetski on February 2, 1927, at St. Vincent's
Hospital in Philadelphia, The Getz family first settled in Philadelphia
But during the Depression the family moved to New York City
Seeking better employment opportunities

Getz worked hard in school, Getz's major interest was in musical
Instruments and he played a number of them before his father bought
Him his first saxophone at the age of 13, he attended James Monroe
High School in the Bronx, in 1941, he was accepted into the All City
High School Orchestra of New York City, this gave him a chance to
Receive private, free tutoring from the New York Philharmonic's
Simon Kovar, a bassoon player, he also continued playing the saxophone
He eventually dropped out of school in order to pursue his musical career

In 1943 at the age of 16 he was accepted into Jack Teagarden's band
And because of his age he became Teagarden's ward, Getz also played
Along with Nat King Cole and Lionel Hampton, after playing for Stan Kenton
Jimmy Dorsey, and Benny Goodman, Getz was a soloist with Woody Herman
From 1947 to 1949 in "The Second Herd", and he first gained wide attention
As one of the band's saxophonists, who were known collectively as the
Four Brothers, the others being Serge Chaloff, Zoot Sims and Herbie Steward

During the early '50s, Getz broke away from the Lester Young style to form
His own musical identity, and he was soon among the most popular of all jazzmen
He formed an exciting quintet that co-featured guitarist Jimmy Raney
Their interplay on up-tempo tunes and tonal blend on ballads were quite memorable
Getz helped usher in the bossa nova era by recording Jazz Samba with Charlie Byrd
Their rendition of "*Desafinado*" was a big hit, during the next year, Getz made bossa
Nova-flavored albums with Gary McFarland's big band, Luiz Bonfá, and Laurindo
Almeida, but it was Getz/Gilberto, a collaboration with Antonio Carlos Jobim and
João Gilberto that was his biggest seller, thanks in large part to "*The Girl from
Ipanema*" Featuring the vocals of Astrud, and João Gilberto

In 1987, Getz had a large tumor removed from behind his heart, subsequent tests
Revealed that he had liver cancer and cirrhosis, due to years of substance abuse
Undeterred, Getz embarked on a strict, herbal-based diet hoping to treat the
lymphoma

By fall 1988, MRI scans revealed that the tumor had dramatically shrunken in size
Buoyed by the good news, Getz remained active, touring with pianist Kenny Barron
recording the albums *Apasionado* with Herb Alpert and *You Gotta Pay the Band*
With vocalist Abbey Lincoln, sadly, Getz's cancer never fully abated and he died on
June 6, 1991 at age 64.

SWING, HARD BOP, BOP & BEBOP

George Shearing

Sir George Shearing, born August 1919, was a British jazz pianist
Who for many years led a popular jazz group that recorded for
Discovery Records, MGM Records and Capitol Records, He was
The composer of over 300 titles, including the jazz standard
Lullaby of Birdland, born in Battersea, London, he was born blind
To working class parents, his father delivered coal and his mother
Cleaned trains in the evening, he started to learn piano at the age of
Three and began formal training at Linden Lodge School for the Blind
Where he spent four years

Though he was offered several scholarships, Shearing opted to perform
At a local pub, the Masons Arms in Lambeth, for "25 bob a week" playing
Piano and accordion, he joined an all-blind band during that time and was
Influenced by the records of Teddy Wilson and Fats Waller, in 1940
Shearing joined Harry Parry's popular band and contributed to the comeback
Of Stéphane Grappelli

In 1947, Shearing immigrated to the United States, where his harmonically
Complex style mixing swing, bop and modern classical influences gained
Popularity, he performed with the Oscar Pettiford Trio and led his own jazz
Quartet, recorded for Discovery, Savoy and MGM, including the immensely
Popular single *September in the Rain,* which sold over 900,000 copies
In 1970, he began to phase out his by-now-predictable quintet and disbanded
The group in 1978, Shearing remained fit and active well into his later years
And continued to perform, He never forgot his native country and, in his last
Years, would split his year between living in New York and Chipping Campden
Gloucestershire, where he bought a house

He was appointed Order of the British Empire (OBE) in 1996. In 2007, he was
Knighted. "So", he noted later, "The poor, blind kid from Battersea became
Sir George Shearing, now that's a fairy tale come true." he suffered a
fall at his home and retired from regular performing, George
Shearing died 14 February 2011.

HORACE MUNGIN

Pharaoh Sanders

"Trane was the Father, Pharaoh was the Son, I am the Holy Ghost,"
Said jazz saxophonist, singer/composer Albert Ayler referring to
Farrell Sanders born on October 13, 1940 in Little Rock, Arkansas
Saxophonist Ornette Coleman once described him as "probably the
Best tenor sax player in the world" - an only child, Sanders began his
Musical career accompanying church hymns on clarinet, Sanders began
Playing the tenor saxophone at Scipio Jones High School in North
Little Rock, the band director, Jimmy Cannon, was also a saxophone
Player, introduced Sanders to jazz, then Cannon left, Sanders
Although still a student, took over as the band director until a
Permanent director could be found, an indication of his musical maturity

After finishing high school in 1959, Sanders moved to Oakland
California, and lived with relatives, he briefly attended Oakland
Junior College and studied art and music, once outside the
Jim Crow South, Sanders could play in both black and white clubs
It was also during this time that he met and befriended John Coltrane
Pharaoh Sanders began his professional career playing tenor saxophone
In Oakland, California, he moved to New York City in 1961 after
Playing with rhythm and blues bands, he received his nickname Pharaoh
From bandleader Sun Ra, with whom he was performing, after moving
To New York, Sanders was destitute, he was often living on the streets
Under stairs, wherever he could find a place to stay, his clothes in tatters
Sun Ra gave him a place to stay, bought him a new pair of green pants
With yellow stripes and encouraged him to use the name Pharaoh
And gradually worked him into the band

Sanders came to greater prominence playing with John Coltrane's band
Starting in 1965, as Coltrane began adopting the avant-garde jazz of
Albert Ayler, Sun Ra and Cecil Taylor, Sanders first performed with
Coltrane on *Ascension* recorded in June 1965, then on their dual-tenor
Recording *Meditations* recorded in November 1965, after this Sanders
Joined Coltrane's final quintet, usually performing very lengthy
Dissonant solos, Coltrane's later style was strongly influenced by Sanders

SWING, HARD BOP, BOP & BEBOP

In 1966 Sanders signed with Impulse and recorded *Tauhid* that same year
His years with Impulse caught the attention of jazz fans, critics, and musicians
Alike, including John Coltrane, Ornette Coleman, and Albert Ayler
Sanders continued to produce his own recordings and also continued to work
With the likes of Alice Coltrane on her *Journey In Satchidananda* album
Although supported by African-American radio, Sanders' brand of free jazz
Became less popular, he continued to explore the music of different cultures
And refine his compositions, he found a permanent home with a small label
Called Theresa in 1987 where he began to diversify his sound, in 2000
Sanders released *Spirits* and, in 2003, a live album titled
The Creator Has a Master Plan.

HORACE MUNGIN

A Tribute to
Teo Macero

The triad, Jing, (energy), Qi, (the flow of energy), and Shen, (spirit), are the Tao of all that is. The fundamental of Taoism is the nature of the universe and in this there can be no light except by comparison with darkness; there can be no joy without the existence of sadness. Every action causes a counter action – all of life is a dichotomy; all distinctions are relative comparisons bound together by their mutual reference. In nature, there are no two-headed coins – love is on the other side of hate. In Taoism, there are no principles to learn, no canons to remember, no rituals to practice. Ultimately, it is useless trying to understand Tao; for it cannot be expressed in words. It is shapeless and formless. It is, what is unknown, but instinctively adhered to.

Yet, the March 1961 Miles Davis recording of "Someday My Prince Will Come" which features a tribute to saxophonist, composer, record producer Teo Macero called simply Teo is, for me, an example of glimpsing the unknowable – an audible revelation of Taoism dichotomy, an exposure to the supreme search being acted out. John Coltrane's solo is so innovative, it's akin to hearing someone pray a prayer that convinces you that it is, at that very moment, being received by divinity.

Mile Davis composed the tune "Teo" in honor of his longtime friend, record producer and fellow musician Attilio Joseph (Teo) Macero. Teo was born October 30, 1925 in Glens Falls, New York and died February 19, 2008 after a long career as a musician, record producer, and film and television soundtrack composer. Teo was a producer at Columbia Records for twenty years and produced the Miles Davis album *Kind of Blue*, which at # 12, is the highest-rank jazz album on *Rolling Stone*'s 500 Greatest Albums of All Time list and is the best-selling jazz album of all time. Teo Macero graduated from the Juilliard School of Music in 1953 with Bachelor's and Master's degrees. Teo also worked with Dave Brubeck, Thelonious Monk, and Charles Mingus. He scored the 1970 Muhammad Ali documentary, aka, Cassius Clay and produced the soundtrack for Martin Scorsese's film *The Blues*.

So, it was fitting that such an accomplished soul was given the tribute that Miles Davis bestowed on his music collaborator and one can only surmise that it was providence that inspired the musicians to such grand heights. This Miles Davis Sextet is comprised of Miles on trumpet, Hank Mobley and John Coltrane on saxophone, Wynton Kelly on piano, Paul chambers on bass, and Billy Cobb on drums – all of whom went on to head bands of their own. There are six tunes on the album which has one of Miles' several wives on the cover. The cut "Teo" which lasts nine minutes and thirty-two seconds is totally enlightening and John Coltrane's solo is its spiritual core.

The tune "Teo" starts with a few bars of a bass introduction then it is joined for a few bars by the entire rhythm section before Miles began the journey with a calm call and answer that slowly evolves into a delightful bounce of notes that dance with themselves. Then there are a series of shape notes that jar the mood, repeat several times and then develop into the resolve of Miles' hymn of preparation. Miles blows a series of defiant images which ends with a series of notes that seem themselves to want to prepare the path to the Way (As in Tao is the Way). All the while, the rhythm section is keeping up a driving orderliness – with special attention to the orderliness as a means to contain within its perimeter what's to come. There is a short rhythm section interlude that builds anticipation before Coltrane burst into consciousness.

And then it happens; John Coltrane enters like a screaming storm, melancholy and self-possessed, pleading for harmonic equality. There are echoes of the turmoil of the times – a musical declaration of freedom – We Shall Overcome. This feeling builds and becomes elaborate, convoluted and twists over and over and turns into repeated screams, and turns dark, then chaotic – and there you have frenzied images bubbling within the framed orderliness of the rhythm section. It is here that the sacred happens, a chaotic tidiness that is the oxymoron of Taoism infused into this tribute to Teo and links itself to the search for the mathematical equation physics seek that would reconcile Albert Einstein's harmonic General Theory of Evolution with the anarchic reality of Quantum Mechanics, that's called the String Theory – The Theory of Everything. And listening to Coltrane there is no stretch between the search for the Taoism Way and the search for either the string theory or the righteousness of black Americans' quest for social justice. They are all expeditions to awareness.

Coltrane is still blowing.

When I first heard this recording in 1962, at the age of 19, I identified it with the movement towards social justice that was taking place in the streets. To me, it sounded like a fitting exhortation for the energy of Malcolm X or an anthem for the Black Panthers. As I grew older and became armed with other knowledge, I realized that there was also something more universal going on in this music. These cats were visionaries, far ahead of me – they could combine the contemporary with future expectations and talk about comprehending the cosmos – a thing far in the future, and a thing that had as much to do with the nature of Taoism as it had to do with the String Theory of Everything. Understanding is at the core of every quest.

Coltrane is breaking free of the turmoil and glides down to earthly realities where Miles can handle the transfer. Miles comes on exhausted from the energy spent translating the logic of Coltrane's solo and it takes a few bars for him to regain, once again, the confidence of his own instincts which now collaborates with, or, may even now be born from the Coltrane performance - it is all one now and when Miles blows his last note, the rhythm section, alone, closed the curtains.

Chinua Achebe, the Nigerian author and teacher wrote once, that he "seek to do with the English language what African American jazz musician had done with European instruments – mold and bend them until these instruments could tell their saga in an epic universal language." Nowhere in the annals of music is that statement clearer than in John Coltrane's performance in "Teo".

Reviews on "Swing, Hard Bop, Bop and Be Bop: Biographical Jazz Prose Poems" by Horace Mungin...

HORACE MUNGIN

Jack Magnus
5-Star Review for Readers Favorite, LLC

"Swing, Hard Bop, Bop & Bebop: Biographical Jazz Prose Poems" is a nonfiction music/entertainment book written by Horace Mungin. Mungin is a poet and author, who has written a number of biographical works on jazz artists. As his About the Author page indicates, he grew up in San Juan Hill, an area in New York City, which could be considered the birthplace of jazz in all its incarnations and subtleties. It was not uncommon for children growing up in his neighborhood to hear the sounds of Thelonious Monk and other jazz musicians wafting from overhead as they played in school yards. He and his peers knew intimately and first-hand which musicians were in town, and who would be playing in Birdland. Mungin's introduction sets the stage for the biographical poems that follow. He discusses the beginnings of African-American music in those early work songs of the slave laborers, which evolved into spirituals and often included coded messages about escape routes. As a child, Mungin also wanted to be a musician, and like his peers, chose his own instrument, a flute which he mainly learned by practicing along with recordings. He was not, by any means, alone in being predominantly self-taught. Many of the musicians he highlights in this work learned from what they heard and then used their own creative flair to build on what became a rich and vibrant tapestry.

I will admit to having familiarity with far too few of the musicians showcased in Horace Mungin's collection of biographical poetry, which made reading his book all the more intriguing and illuminating. There's the saying that a little knowledge can be more dangerous than ignorance, but my scant acquaintance with Coltrane, Rollins and other jazz greats made me even more curious about who they were and how jazz, as I was familiar with it, came to be, how "New Music in America" got its start and what its history was. Mungin's poems are brilliant, insightful and eloquent. They're also highly accessible and very easy to read. Anyone who hesitates in reading this book because of the dreaded word "poems" should sit down and experience what a poet of Mungin's caliber can actually do. His prose poems flow beautifully, and under his deft touch each of the jazz musicians highlighted comes to life, shares their story and passes the torch on to the next artist. I learned so much reading this book, and I found it was impossible to put down. "Swing, Hard Bop, Bop & Bebop: Biographical Jazz Prose Poems" is an educational experience that would be a grand basis for a series of academic courses on the subject. This illuminating and enlightening work is most highly recommended.

SWING, HARD BOP, BOP & BEBOP

Osei T. Chandler
Producer/Host: Roots Musik Karamu
South Carolina Public Radio
Weekend Host, Jazz works – (Syndicated)

This book is as great a reading for the jazz aficionado as it is for the casual listener! Filled with tib-bits and anecdotes, biographical data and historical facts, this collection of 60 prose poems assembled in 'Swing, Hard Bop, Bop and Bebop' is informational, inspirational and seriously entertaining! Horace Mungin is, at times, a reporter on the scene; at other times, a poet tour guide down memory lane into a special time and place in music history.

These poetic essays provide insights and reflections on many of the icons in the world of music. Mungin's writing is descriptive and often lyrical, sometimes mimicking the solos of the musicians. The essays provide a resource for research as they shine light on the artists, the times, and events and even a few venues (think Jazz Mobile and Amateur Night at the Apollo).

Horace Mungin shines a light on the styles and approaches of several artists with an improvisational touch: Regarding Thelonious Monk - "…uses silence and hesitation;" Charlie Parker - "As sloppy with his life as he was flawless with his music;" Oscar Peterson – "The Maharaja of the piano;" Lester Young "had a tone all his own." Pure jazz as poetry!

As you read, you will bear witness to interactions and conversations that tickle your funny bone, jerk tears from your heart, provoke a smile or even a belly laugh. Pick up this read and share Horace Mungin's joy and appreciation of the music. As Horace says, "It's the next best thing to being there!"

It truly is.

HORACE MUNGIN

Quentin E Baxter (BME, LLC)
Musician/Producer/Educator

"Swing, Hard Bop, Bob & Bebop" is a refreshing outlook on many important key "players" responsible for the bebop era of jazz music. From the innovative musicians who created this distinct mode of expression, to the producers and advocates who played important roles in making it possible to experience and preserve the sheer genius of this expression.

I, like many musicians of my generation, am too young to have stomped around NYC during the bebop era. "Swing, Hard Bop, Bop & Bebop" is definitely a testimony of one who loves, respects, and still lives the "vibe & culture" of the bebop era. Luckily for us, this testimony is expressed and preserved in a way that keeps it conversational. While reading, you'll get an accurate sense of rhythm and flow from someone uniquely influenced by the music, the musicians, the architects and advocates, and "vibe & culture" of bebop.

About the Author

Horace Mungin grew up in San Juan Hill, in New York City. It is a neighborhood with a long involvement in the creation, celebration and unconventional embracing of music – jazz music – and Thelonious Monk lived there. The young boys on the basketball court heard Monk and Charlie Rouse rehearsing live some Saturday mornings as their music sailed from Monk's open window at 238 West 63rd Street over to the basketball court around the corner and they often saw jazz musicians in the neighborhood on their way to Monk's crib. Other teens collected baseball cards and kept up on hit/run statistics; Mungin's clique collected jazz facts; what musicians were in town and who was at Birdland, and who was playing Grant's Tomb on the Jazz Mobile. They knew the list of sidemen; they knew who played bass or drums with which major headliner. Mungin has turned that experience and a life-time of collecting jazz music and jazz facts into a series of succinct biographical guides of swing and bebop artists for all jazz fans to savor.

HORACE MUNGIN

SWING, HARD BOP, BOP & BEBOP